33
DAYS *to*
EUCHARISTIC
GLORY

BLUE
sparrow

ISBN: 978-1-63582-532-9 (softcover)
ISBN: 978-1-63582-513-8 (hardcover)
ISBN: 978-1-63582-525-1 (eBook)
Audiobook available from Audible.

33 DAYS to EUCHARISTIC GLORY
may be purchased for groups large and small.
For information, please call or email:
info@DynamicCatholic.com
1-859-980-7700
www.DynamicCatholic.com

International and foreign rights are available for this title.
For information, please email info@Viident.com
www.Viident.com

Designed by Todd Detering

10 9 8 7 6 5 4 3 2 1

FIRST EDITION

Printed in the United States of America

TABLE OF CONTENTS

THE FINAL DAYS: THE MOMENT OF SURRENDER

APPENDIX:

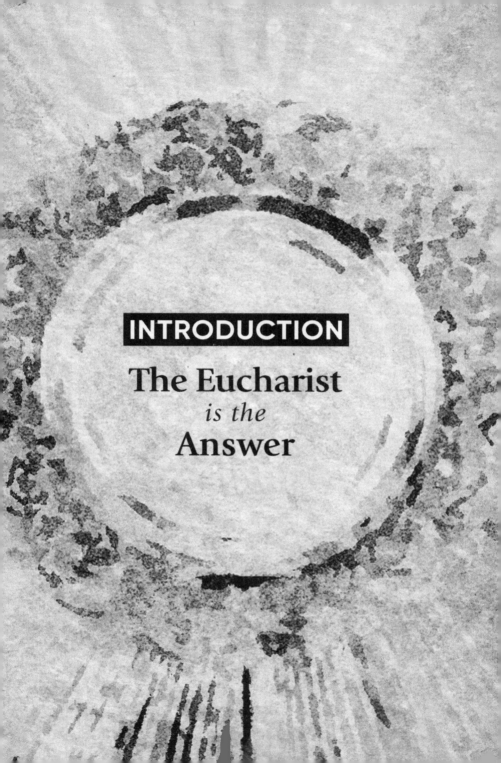

INTRODUCTION

The Eucharist
is the
Answer

"I HAVE A DREAM. . ."

These are among the most quoted words in the English language outside of the Bible. They are the words of Martin Luther King Jr. If he had stood on the steps of the Lincoln Memorial on that hot summer's day in 1963 and said, "I have a plan," would the speech have become one of the most memorable speeches of all time? I don't think so.

The ability to dream is uniquely human and an extraordinary gift. This God-given ability to look into the future and imagine something better, then return to the present and work to bring about that better future, is remarkable. And yet, sadly, it is massively underemployed in most people's lives.

Think on it for a moment. When was the last time you used your God-given ability to chase down a personal dream? When was the last time, together as Catholics, we had a common dream and pursued it with relentless passion?

I believe it is time we all started dreaming again. I realize the first response of many will be to tell us why it won't work before we have even begun. But it is time to move beyond this defeatism and dream again as Catholics. Where are the possibility thinkers of our age? Will you be one? This is a time for Catholics to start dreaming, to envision bold possibilities, and to work together in collaboration with God to make those dreams a reality.

So, let me tell you a little about my dream, and then perhaps it can become our dream.

I have a dream that the whole world would be consecrated to the Eucharist.

One person at a time,
one marriage at a time,
one family at a time,
one neighborhood at a time,
one parish at a time,
one diocese at a time,
one country at a time.

The whole world consecrated to Jesus in the Eucharist.
Join me in this dream and together we can do something bold and visionary. It is a bold dream. But isn't that what is needed? "Be bold and mighty forces will come to your aid," was Goethe's insight. Those mighty forces are Father, Son, Holy Spirit, and all their angels and saints. Isn't it time Catholics did something bold?

It is my fervent hope that my dream will help fuel your dreams and together as Catholics we will become a people of possibility again.

WHAT IS CONSECRATION?

Consecration is to devote yourself to God and make yourself 100 percent available to carry out His will on this earth. It is an act of unconditional surrender to God. Through the act of consecration, we dedicate ourselves abundantly, wholeheartedly, and completely to the will of God, surrender our distractions and selfishness, and promise to faithfully respond to God's grace in our lives.

In the Book of Exodus, after the incident with the golden calf, Moses realized that the people had lost their way, and so he called them together and said, "Consecrate yourselves today to the Lord... that He may bestow upon you a blessing this day." (Exodus 32:29)

In the First Book of Chronicles, after God chose his son Solomon to lead, David gave everything he had over to God and the people of Israel. And then he asked, "Who else among you will contribute generously and consecrate themselves to the Lord this day?" (1 Chronicles 29:5)

In the Book of Joshua, God's chosen people entered the Promised Land after wandering in the desert for forty years. Joshua asked the priests to carry the Ark of the Covenant before the people and said, "Consecrate yourselves to the Lord, for tomorrow He will do wonders among you." (Joshua 3:5) For the Jewish people, the Ark of the Covenant was God's dwelling place on earth, God's presence among them.

The Eucharist is God dwelling among us. And so, today I say to you, with Moses, David, and Joshua:

"Consecrate yourselves today to the Lord . . . that He may bestow upon you a blessing this day."

"Who else among you will contribute generously and consecrate themselves to the Lord this day?"

"Consecrate yourselves to the Lord, for tomorrow He will do wonders among you."

33 Days to Eucharistic Glory is the first ever guide to Eucharistic Consecration. Catholics have consecrated themselves to the Immaculate Heart of Mary, to the Sacred Heart of Jesus, to Saint Joseph, Saint Raphael, Saint Michael the Archangel, Saint Anne, the Holy Spirit, the Miraculous Medal, Our Lady of Guadalupe, the Mediatrix of All Grace, Our Lady of Fatima, Our Lady of Lourdes, Our Lady of Czestochowa, Our Lady of Mount Carmel, Our Lady of Sorrows, and to the Holy Trinity.

I believe it is time we consecrated ourselves to Jesus in the Eucharist—it is time for a Eucharistic Consecration.

THE INCREDIBLE JOURNEY BEFORE YOU

You are about to embark on an incredible journey. This isn't just another book. It is an invitation to participate in a sacred journey—a spiritual pilgrimage. It's a guide that will lead you to the essence of what it means to be Catholic . . . and it will change your life in the most marvelous of ways.

Eucharistic Consecration will take your spiritual life to unimaginable new levels, but it will also energize the way you participate in relationships; ignite a new curiosity about yourself and others; transform the way you think about money and things; refocus your professional life; liberate you from many of your fears, doubts, and anxieties; make you aware of the hopes and dreams God has placed in your heart; and breathe new life into your appreciation for the genius of Catholicism.

Along the way you will meet many people who desperately need what you are holding in your hands right now. I hope you will share it with them. By sharing this Eucharistic way with them, you will become a Eucharistic Missionary, preparing their hearts for Jesus to enter and transform their lives.

CRISIS OF FAITH

The Catholic Church in America has been in crisis for decades. This is an uncomfortable truth, but one that will not change unless we face it.

Modern Catholics are experiencing a crisis of faith. Materialism and secularism have been eroding the faith of Catholics for decades. The result is most starkly recognized in the research that shows only 31 percent of Catholics in the United States believe Jesus is truly present in the Eucharist. Here are a few more statistics that reveal the depth and breadth of this crisis:

- More than fifty million Catholics in the United States have stopped practicing their faith over the past thirty years.
- More than half of all American adults raised Catholic (52 percent) have now left the Church. Only 8 percent say returning to the Catholic Church is something they could imagine doing.
- We have closed a Catholic parish in the United States every three days for the past thirty-five years.
- We have closed a Catholic school in the United States every four days for the past twenty-five years.
- Over the past fifty years we have lost a Catholic priest from active service every day in the United States due to retirement, death, men who have left the priesthood voluntarily or those who have been removed.
- In 1973 there were 58,000 priests in the United States, the average age was thirty-five, and only 10 percent were over the age of sixty-five. Today there are 37,000 priests in the United States, the average age is sixty-four, and 40 percent are over the age of sixty-five.
- 3,500 parishes in the United States are now without a resident priest.

These numbers are real, but statistics are cold. Behind each of these vast numbers is a human being, and a soul, and a family, often a marriage, and more often than that, parents who suffer wondering why their child no longer goes to Mass and what went wrong along the way.

We have all been impacted personally by these statistics. But there is another aspect for us to keep in mind as we chart a path forward. I tried to capture it more than twenty years ago, in the opening line of the first edition of *Rediscover Catholicism*: "The Church (like so many other things in life) is not so much something we inherit from generations past, or take over from our predecessors, as it is something on loan to us from future generations."

The Catholic Church is on loan to us from future generations. The negative trends above are only part of the picture. Wherever the Catholic faith is authentically lived out, the genius of Catholicism still has the power to attract people of all ages and help them make sense of life.

In 2014 in the United States there were 708,979 infant baptisms, 44,544 adult baptisms, and 70,117 adults received into Full Communion. Even more encouraging is the data which shows that 43 percent of people who consider themselves cultural-Catholics (Catholic but not practicing) say they can imagine returning to the Catholic Church in the future.

We need to forge the kind of future that will bring them back.

It is easy to be critical, and it is even easier to become overwhelmed by the challenges we face. But we all have some responsibility here, and we all have a role to play in renewing the Church in our place and time. In order to reflect upon our role and responsibility, I invite you to reflect upon this question: There are 1.2 billion Catholics on the planet: What would the Catholic Church be like if we multiplied your life by 1.2 billion?

Catholicism has not lost its power to transform lives. Yet, people are abandoning Catholicism at an alarming rate in Europe and the United States, and this is not a new trend. And so, I raise the question: What are we going to do about it?

The key to answering that question is one piece of data that is more significant than all the data we have reflected upon collectively so far.

(Sources: Pew Research Center, USCCB, CARA, The Dynamic Catholic Institute, and U.S. Census Bureau. Where data is not current year, the year shown is the latest data available).

THOSE WHO BELIEVE DON'T LEAVE

What is the difference between the people who have left the Catholic Church over the past thirty years and those who have stayed? I believe the answer to this question holds the key to re-energizing the Catholic Church.

It would be easy to escape into the complexity of this issue and say there are many differences. We have spent the last thirty years lost down that rabbit hole. It is true. There are many differences between these two groups, but it is equally true, more so in fact, that one difference marks the essential difference between the fifty million people who have left the Catholic Church over the past thirty years and those who have stayed.

What is the one thing? What is this essential difference?

Those who believe don't leave. Believe what? Believe that Jesus is truly present in the Eucharist.

Those who believe this single truth may feel like they are not being fed, they may disagree with the way their priest is doing things, they may not like the direction the music is moving in, they may have different liturgical preferences, they may get divorced, and they may feel unseen and unwelcome in their parish community. And yet, despite all these things that have led millions of people to leave, they stay. Why? They believe Jesus Christ is truly present in the Eucharist and they know that only the Catholic Church can offer this gift to them. They might be able to go down the road and experience better preaching and more dynamic music, but they are simply not willing to give up the Eucharist in exchange for that. Why? Because it's a bad deal. But you have to know and believe that Jesus is truly present in the Eucharist to understand how bad a deal it is to give that up for what is trivial by comparison.

Those who believe don't leave. This one piece of data is

more significant than all the other data combined.

Those who believe don't leave. This single truth holds the power to change everything.

The most effective way to slow and halt the exodus the Catholic Church is experiencing in the United States is to lead people to believe in the True Presence of Jesus in the Eucharist. And the most effective way to bring people back to the Catholic Church will be by leading them to believe that Jesus is present in the Eucharist. And the most effective way to attract people to Catholicism who have never even considered becoming Catholic is by facilitating for them powerful encounters with Jesus Christ who lives among us today in the Eucharist.

We all know plenty of people who have left the Church, and even more who have simply stopped practicing the faith. But how many people do you know who have left the Catholic Church who believe in the True Presence? None I suspect. I don't know any. And herein lies the answer. If we yearn to re-energize the Catholic Church in America, if we want to bring our friends and family home, if we want to spare future generations the pain and confusion that comes from leaving the Church—the Eucharist is the answer. Specifically, powerful encounters that inspire belief in the True Presence of Jesus Christ—Body, Blood, Soul, and Divinity—in the Eucharist.

This is the one thing: the Eucharist. Jesus present in our tabernacles and monstrances, Jesus waiting to give Himself to us in Communion during the Holy Sacrifice of the Mass.

Those who believe don't leave. It's the one simple beautiful truth that will change everything.

WHAT MAKES CATHOLICISM UNIQUE?

There are 45,000 different denominations of Christianity in the world. What is the one thing that makes the Catholic Church unique?

"It's not just one thing," some people will argue, "Many things make Catholicism unique." They are right. But what one thing differentiates Catholicism more than anything else? What is the principal differentiator between the Catholic Church and the churches on every other street corner?

The Eucharist. Jesus Christ—the King of Kings, the Lord of Lords, the Alpha and the Omega—truly present—Body, Blood, Soul, and Divinity—in the Eucharist. He is the difference.

"Transforming people one at a time is at the heart of God's plan for the world." This is the opening line of *The Four Signs of a Dynamic Catholic*. It is also the key to solving the problems we face as a Church today. God doesn't transform parishes, businesses, schools, or countries. God transforms people, and He does it one at a time. He then collaborates with those He has transformed to continue the process. The outcome of these individual transformations is that marriages, families, parishes, businesses, communities, schools, and countries are transformed. But God's primary purpose is never the transformation of an organization or even a group of people. Our God is a deeply personal God, and He takes a deeply personal interest in each person.

Over the next thirty-three days I believe you will become well and truly convinced that a renewed relationship with Jesus in the Eucharist can be transformational.

Re-energizing the Catholic Church in America will be achieved not by finding an idea or program that transforms thousands of people at a time. It will be achieved one person at a time.

THE EUCHARIST IS THE ANSWER

For twenty-five years, between 1993 and 2018, I traveled hundreds of days each year visiting parishes and speaking at conferences around the world. During that time, I visited more than 3,000 Catholic parishes in the United States to speak.

From my earliest days on the road, I recognized a pattern, a phenomenon—an observable fact—that demonstrated new life could be breathed into parishes and explained how it was happening. That phenomenon was Perpetual Adoration Chapels. It wasn't just an idea. It was living and breathing. It had been implemented in lots of communities and was bearing abundant fruit.

There is something powerful about giving people a quiet place to spend time with God. These peaceful places of refuge from the busyness of life and noise of the world were a soothing balm for parishioners' souls. They provided a place to reestablish priorities. It was somewhere to focus on what matters most in a world driven mad with distractions. A place simply to be with Jesus.

Did I notice other initiatives having powerful renewal effects in parishes? Yes, another trend I noticed was the outsized impact Christ Renews His Parish was having on parish renewal. But nothing was more powerful than the impact I saw Perpetual Adoration Chapels having on parishes.

But it isn't enough just to build an Adoration Chapel. The introduction of an Adoration Chapel into a parish was more successful in some places than in others. Why?

Those parishes that were most positively impacted by an Adoration Chapel were those that had an active ministry surrounding it. Those standout parishes were dedicated to inviting and encouraging new people to participate every month. They tried to get everyone in the parish involved in some way, rather than having the same few people who do everything in the parish sign up for the time slots and then putting it on autopilot.

I have seen so many lives transformed by Perpetual Adoration Chapels. Those people then engage in their marriage, family, work, and parish on a whole new level as a result, continuing the ripple effect of Christ's presence in the world.

We shouldn't be surprised. It shouldn't be a grand revelation. It should be obvious. Give people the chance to spend time in the presence of Jesus and their lives will be changed.

It's simple. It's beautiful. And it works. Give people the chance to spend time in the presence of Jesus and their lives will be changed.

All those years I spent on the road I saw more proof of this phenomenon at youth gatherings. Get 1,000 young people together, 2,000, 5,000. Turn the lights off, light some candles, and set Jesus in the monstrance in an elevated place in the middle of those young people. There is complete silence. Their souls cherish the silence to reflect upon their lives. And one experience like that can convince a person to make time for quiet prayer and reflection every day for the rest of their lives.

We need to create more unique opportunities for people to encounter Jesus.

Do the same thing at World Youth Day in Denver, Manila, Sydney, Paris, Rome, Madrid, Rio de Janeiro, Krakow, Lisbon—with hundreds of thousands of young people, and the impact is overwhelming. Five million young people gathered for World Youth Day in Luneta Park in Manila, Philippines, leading Guinness World Records to recognize it as the largest crowd for a live event in human history. Five million people in contemplative silence amidst a world gone mad. It was awe-inspiring.

Many people encounter Jesus for the first time in their lives in Adoration. This is where they have their first deeply personal experience of Jesus. They may have heard about Jesus their whole lives, they may have been receiving Jesus in the Eucharist every Sunday, but there is something about the experience of Jesus in Adoration that leads people to know Him. This shift from knowing about Jesus to knowing Jesus changes everything.

And once they are awakened in this way, the Holy Spirit leads them to live their faith and participate in all types of ministries. This is where we begin to see the differences between highly engaged Catholics and disengaged Catholics. The more disengaged a Catholic is, the more they treat the faith like a consumer. More engaged Catholics take on the heart and mind of a disciple, constantly looking for ways to share the joy they have found with everyone who crosses their path in life.

I have become convinced that the renewal of the Catholic Church will be a Eucharistic renewal, or there will be no renewal at all. There is simply no other way.

The world has many problems. The Church has many problems. You have many. I have many. Is it possible that the Eucharist is the answer to all our problems? Could it be so gloriously simple? Let's find out together.

HOW TO USE THIS BOOK

Over the next thirty-three days you are going to take a spiritual pilgrimage. Some people go on pilgrimage to the Holy Land, Fatima, Lourdes, Santiago de Compostela or Rome. I hope you can join us one day on one of our amazing pilgrimages to these places. But this spiritual pilgrimage you can make in the comfort of your favorite chair. And yet, it will be the longest journey you ever make without moving an inch.

A pilgrimage is a sacred journey with a specific intention. Our journey will be an inner journey, and our specific intention is Eucharistic Consecration.

This book is intended as a handbook for your spiritual pilgrimage. The readings, prayers, and other resources are arranged day-by-day and under a weekly theme. This is a time of preparation for the profound experience of Eucharistic Consecration. The reflections are designed to be deeply spiritual and intensely practical.

This preparation will require about fifteen minutes each day. Here is a step-by-step guide to each day:

1. Find a quiet place.
2. Read the reflection.
3. Ponder the one idea that struck you most from the reading for a few minutes.
4. Pray the Spiritual Communion.
5. Look for opportunities to adopt the virtue of the day amidst your daily activities.
6. Have a great day!

The journey will last thirty-three days. Four weeks and five days. Each week is arranged around a theme and designed to prepare you for your consecration on day thirty-three, but also to educate and inspire you about the extraordinary power of the Eucharist.

Week One:	The Eucharist and the Pilgrim
Week Two:	The Eucharist and the Saints
Week Three:	The Eucharist and You
Week Four:	The Eucharist and History
The Final Days:	The Moment of Surrender

If you miss a day, don't get discouraged, and don't quit. Every evil force in the universe wants you to do that. You will feel the pull of those evil spirits at times. And the pull of those evil spirits will be tempting you to abandon this pilgrimage. Don't. See those temptations for what they are: proof that what you are doing is a powerful spiritual exercise that is going to bear abundant fruit in your life and for the world.

If you miss a day, or two days, or even five days, do not give in to discouragement. Discouragement doesn't come from God.

If you miss days, simply read the days you missed, and keep moving forward. You will be tempted to abandon this journey or tempted to go back and start again. Don't. This again is just the pull of evil spirits that do not want you to complete this consecration.

If you started praying the rosary and started over each time you got distracted, you would never finish a single rosary.

Stay the course. Don't give in to distraction or discouragement. No matter what, thirty-three days after you start: Consecrate yourself to Jesus in the Eucharist. Day 33 lays out clearly how to complete the Act of Consecration.

All that's left to do now is select a start date. You can start your spiritual pilgrimage any day you wish. It is, however, tradition to begin on a date that leads you to complete the consecration on a feast day. With that in mind, you will find a chart at the end of this section of with some options for starting your journey. More options are available at the website Eucharist.us.

But keep in mind that the Church honors at least one saint or solemnity every day of the year. Some people like to conclude on the feast day of their favorite saint or the saint they were named after. And if you wish to start today, it is just a matter of calculating which feast day will be your day of consecration. I do think it is good to know before you begin, so call on that saint's intercession along the way, especially during moments of difficulty and discouragement.

LET THE PILGRIMAGE BEGIN

As you set off on your pilgrimage, let me share a short story. Many years ago, I met a Muslim man. We were working together on a project, and we came to know each other. I asked him questions about his faith, and he asked me questions about Christianity and Catholicism. This went on for over two years until the project was finished. Throughout this time, there was one question I wanted to ask him but had held back.

On the last day of the project there was a little downtime in the afternoon and Providence opened a door.

"Can I ask you one more question about your faith?" I began.

"Sure. Anything," he replied.

"We have spoken about Catholic belief surrounding the Eucharist. So, I was wondering, if you believed you could consume Allah under the guise of bread, what would you be willing to do in order to receive such bread?"

He looked at me for a long time. It might have been five minutes. It felt like an hour. At first, I thought I may have offended him in some way. But he was a man of deep thought and it became clear he was seriously considering my question.

Then a look came over his face, he cleared his throat, and he said, "If I believed as you described, I would crawl naked over red-hot broken glass to receive such bread."

Quite a contrast to how disrespected the Eucharist is by so many Catholics today.

Over the next thirty-three days I will be praying and fasting for you. I pray it will be a profound and deeply mystical journey. May the Eucharistic Glory of Jesus Christ find a home deep in your soul and remain with you forever.

Jesus waits for you in the Eucharist, in our tabernacles and monstrances, and on the altar at every Mass. His message to you is unmistakable. In a world where so many people feel unseen, unheard, and unworthy, Jesus generously proclaims: *I see you. I hear you. I know you. You are worthy. I am with you. I care. I am yours. You are Mine.* And this is His invitation: "Come to me, all you that are weary and are carrying heavy burdens, and I will give you rest." (Matthew 11:28)

Go to Him. Seek out time in His presence. Allow His presence to transform you in ways unimaginable.

Matthew Kelly

2024

BEGIN PREPARATION	FEAST OF JESUS	CONSECRATION/ FEAST DAY
January 1	The Presentation of the Lord	February 2
February 21	Palm Sunday	March 24
February 26	Good Friday	March 29
February 28	Easter	March 31
March 6	Divine Mercy Sunday	April 7
April 10	The Ascension of the Lord	May 12
April 24	Trinity Sunday	May 26
May 1	Corpus Christi	June 2
May 6	Feast of the Sacred Heart of Jesus	June 7
July 5	The Transfiguration of the Lord	August 6
August 13	The Exaltation of the Holy Cross	September 14
October 23	Solemnity of Christ the King	November 24
November 23	Christmas	December 25
November 27	The Holy Family of Jesus, Mary, and Joseph	December 29
December 4, 2024	The Epiphany of the Lord	January 5, 2025
December 11, 2024	The Baptism of the Lord	January 12, 2025

WEEK ONE

The Eucharist
and the
Pilgrim

JUST PASSING THROUGH
DAY 1

"This is the day the Lord has made, let us rejoice and be glad."
Psalm 118:24

For thousands of years, men and women of every age, race, and culture have sought to understand the meaning of life. The people of our own time are no different.

Throughout history, scientists and philosophers, theologians and artists, politicians and social activists, monks and sages, and men and women from all walks of life have discussed and debated many questions in the quest to discover the meaning of life. And while their discussions have been many and varied, all of humanity's searching for answers can be arranged under five questions.

These are the five questions that humanity has been asking consciously and subconsciously since the beginning of human history. Although we may be unable to articulate them, you and I are constantly asking these questions in our daily lives. Whether we are aware of it or not, our whole existence is a searching to answer these five questions. We seek the answers to these questions directly and indirectly every day. And how we answer these questions determines the shape, form, and direction that our lives take. These are the five questions every heart longs to answer:

1. Who am I?
2. Where did I come from?
3. What am I here for?
4. How do I do it?
5. Where am I going?

Our journey together will answer these questions. It will be a journey from confusion to clarity, a journey from chaos to order. Over the next thirty-three days you will get clear about what matters most and what doesn't matter much at all. This clarity will be liberating and invigorating.

The wisdom of the young and innocent is unmatched. My five-year-old son Ralph came into my study one day last week to say goodnight. I gave him a huge hug and a kiss, and said, "You are delicious, Ralphie. I love you for two forevers."

"No Daddy," he replied.

"What do you mean?" I inquired.

"There is only one forever, Daddy," he said with great confidence.

"Really?" I questioned again.

"Yes, this life is not forever. We are only passing through this world. The only forever is in Heaven with God."

Let's take a moment and sit with that. This is coming from a five-year-old. "This life is not forever. We are just passing through this world." Powerful! And it is a great place to begin our thirty-three-day journey together.

The truth: We are all just passing through this world.

We are pilgrims. Life is a pilgrimage. It is a sacred journey toward a very specific destination. But we forget this, or have never been taught it, or we get distracted and fall into thinking we are tourists. We aren't. We are pilgrims.

For thousands of years, men and women of all faiths have been making pilgrimages. These sacred journeys are powerful experiences that people make in search of God, His will, and His favor. Most of all, these sacred journeys remind us that life itself is a pilgrimage, and that we are just passing through this place we call Earth.

Over the past thirty years, I have been exceedingly fortunate to have had the opportunity to visit many sacred sites. I have visited Fatima more than twenty-five times, Rome and Assisi dozens of times, the Holy Land to walk where Jesus walked and witnessed the Gospels come alive like never before, and have walked the

Camino twice. On these sacred journeys, traveling with pilgrims from all walks of life, I have witnessed thousands of people have life-altering experiences and I have been personally transformed.

I have also made pilgrimages to my local parish, the parish of my childhood, and the cathedrals and basilicas of countless cities around the world.

A pilgrimage doesn't need to be an international adventure. And while I hope someday you can join my colleagues at Dynamic Catholic on one of our extraordinary pilgrimages, it is crucial that we understand that this thirty-three-day journey we are embarking on together is an equally powerful pilgrimage experience.

When I do travel on pilgrimages with groups, I always gather the pilgrims together on the first evening, after a long day of travel, to focus their hearts on two thoughts.

This is the first. Life is a pilgrimage, but sometimes we need a pilgrimage to rediscover life. Sacred journeys focus our hearts, minds, bodies, and souls on what matters most. This journey from confusion to clarity allows us to live more fully than ever before with passion and purpose.

This is the second. Are you going to be a pilgrim or a tourist?

Tomorrow we will explore the difference between pilgrims and tourists. Today, let us be mindful that we are setting off on a journey together. A journey to the Holy of Holies, to the soul of Christ, to Eucharistic Glory.

Just as the Jewish people ate manna from Heaven during their forty years of wandering in the desert before entering The Promised Land, we too eat manna from Heaven during our wanderings on this earth before entering the ultimate promised land in the next life.

The Eucharist is this manna from Heaven. The Eucharist is nourishment for the soul, spiritual food for the journey, that connects us to Heaven (CCC 1402–1405). Each time we receive

Jesus in the Eucharist—Body, Blood, Soul, and Divinity—we touch Heaven. It is this Eucharistic Glory that gives us the patience and courage we need for the sacred pilgrimage we call life.

Trust. Surrender. Believe. Receive.

LESSON
Life is a pilgrimage. We are just passing through this world.

VIRTUE OF THE DAY
Patience: The virtue of patience deepens your ability to meet life's challenges. It is a form of suffering. Though often mild, it does refine character and soul. You can discipline yourself to be patient. This is what the wise and happy do.

SPIRITUAL COMMUNION
Jesus,
I believe that You are truly present
in the Most Holy Sacrament of the Eucharist.
Every day I long for more of You.
I love You above all things, and I desire to receive You into my soul.
Since I cannot receive You sacramentally at this moment,
I invite You to come and dwell in my heart.
May this spiritual communion increase my desire for the Eucharist.
You are the healer of my soul.
Take the blindness from my eyes,
the deafness from my ears,
the darkness from my mind,
and the hardness from my heart.
Fill me with the grace, wisdom, and courage to do Your will in all things.
My Lord and my God, draw me close to You, nearer than ever before.
Amen.

PILGRIM OR TOURIST?
DAY 2

"This is the day the Lord has made, let us rejoice and be glad."
Psalm 118:24

Are you going to be a pilgrim or a tourist on this pilgrimage?

Tourists want everything to go exactly the way they have planned and imagined. Seized by a fear of missing out, they rush around from one place to the next trying to cram everything in. They are constantly buying souvenirs and knickknacks, many of which they will look at when they get home and wonder, "What was I thinking?" Tourists get upset if there are delays. They demand prompt attention and service to all their needs and desires. They focus on themselves, often shoving past others to get where they want to go. Tourists go sightseeing. Tourists calculate the cost.

Pilgrims are very different. They look for signs. If a flight gets delayed or canceled, they ask, "What message is God trying to convey?" Pilgrims are not concerned with seeing and doing everything, just those few things they feel called to. They are not obsessed with shopping. They are aware of the needs of others. Pilgrims go looking for meaning. Pilgrims count their blessings.

The reality is we are all pilgrims. This planet we call Earth is not our home. We are just passing through. If you go on vacation for a week, you don't consider the hotel you stay at to be your home. You know it is a brief stay. In the context of eternity, your life is like that hotel stay. Brief.

We build homes and establish ourselves here on earth in ways that ignore that we are really just here for a short time. It is a dangerous pastime to live as if you were never going to die, but consciously or subconsciously we all fall into this trap to various degrees.

Life is a pilgrimage. What is a pilgrimage? A spiritual journey to a sacred destination. Typically, it is a journey to a shrine or to a location important to a person's faith or beliefs. You can make a pilgrimage to the Holy Land, Rome, Fatima, Lourdes, Santiago de Compostela, or any of the famous Catholic sites around the world. But you could also make a pilgrimage to your nearest cathedral. In fact, every Sunday you make a pilgrimage to your local parish for Mass.

People often make pilgrimages with special intentions in mind. Some ask God for a favor, perhaps to heal a loved one who is sick. Others make a pilgrimage in thanksgiving for a blessing they have already received. Sometimes people make a pilgrimage seeking clarity on some decision they have to make.

There are always couples who come on our trips to celebrate a wedding anniversary. They are making the pilgrimage to thank God for their marriage—the highs and lows, the wonderful memories and the need for forgiveness, the joy and the mess they have muddled through together. And one of the most compelling moments on any Dynamic Catholic pilgrimage is when couples renew their marriage vows. It is powerful in Rome, Assisi, Fatima, Lourdes, Santiago, and it is breathtaking as part of our Mass in Cana on the Holy Land pilgrimage. It's impossible to describe. It is so moving. I have seen it many times, but the impact never fades.

Life is a pilgrimage, but it is easy to get caught up in the things of this world and forget this truth. And that's why sometimes you need a pilgrimage to rediscover the true meaning and purpose of your life.

This life is a journey toward the sacred city, toward the heart of God, toward Eucharistic Glory, toward Heaven. Nobody makes the journey alone. We all need companions. Some of my very best friends in this world I met on pilgrimages. These trips are life-changing, and when you experience something like that with other people, you form a very special bond.

The best friends in the world encourage us and challenge us to become all God created us to be, the-best-version-of-ourselves, and by doing so, they help us to get to Heaven.

Let us pray for the grace to be pilgrims and not just tourists. Let us pray for the grace to be the kind of friend who helps others in the great pilgrimage of life. This is "A Pilgrim's Prayer" by Thomas Merton:

My Lord God,
I have no idea where I am going.
I do not see the road ahead of me.
I cannot know for certain where it will end.
Nor do I really know myself,
And the fact that I think I am following your will
Does not mean that I am actually doing so.
But I believe that the desire to please you,
Does in fact please you.
And I hope I have that desire in all that I am doing.
I hope that I will never do anything apart from that desire.
And I know that if I do this,
You will lead me by the right road, though
I may know nothing about it.
Therefore I will trust you always.
Though I may seem lost in the shadow of death
I will not fear, for you are ever with me,
And you will never leave me to face my perils alone.
Amen.

Now, let me ask you again: Are you a pilgrim or a tourist? This is the quintessential question for anyone setting out on a journey, and a crucial question for our lives. May Jesus in all His Eucharistic Glory share with you the grace to adopt the heart and mind and spirit of a pilgrim, so that you can see, hear, and recognize God's messages along the way. And may the Eucharist provide you with the spiritual sustenance needed to live boldly as a beloved son or daughter of God.

Trust. Surrender. Believe. Receive.

LESSON

A pilgrim awakens each day with a grateful heart and allows God to direct his or her way.

VIRTUE OF THE DAY

Joy: The virtue of joy is a long-lasting state beyond happiness that is not dependent on external circumstances to be sustained. It is possible to be suffering and experience joy at the same time. The flames of joy can be fanned in our hearts with gratitude and service to others. Joy is the fruit of appreciation. If you wish to stir joy in your soul, thank God for all the ways He has blessed you. The other way to flood our souls with joy is by lovingly serving others in need.

SPIRITUAL COMMUNION

Jesus,
I believe that You are truly present
in the Most Holy Sacrament of the Eucharist.
Every day I long for more of You.
I love You above all things, and I desire to receive You into my soul.
Since I cannot receive You sacramentally at this moment,
I invite You to come and dwell in my heart.
May this spiritual communion increase my desire for the Eucharist.
You are the healer of my soul.

Take the blindness from my eyes,
the deafness from my ears,
the darkness from my mind,
and the hardness from my heart.
Fill me with the grace, wisdom, and courage to do Your will in all things.
My Lord and my God, draw me close to You, nearer than ever before.
Amen.

THE FOUR LAST THINGS
DAY 3

"This is the day the Lord has made, let us rejoice and be glad."
Psalm 118:24

For hundreds of years, if you attended a retreat or a parish mission, you didn't have to wonder what the opening topic might be. You would have known. It would have been the Four Last Things. This was always the opening topic. The Four Last Things were also traditionally the topic of homilies preached on the four Sundays of Advent.

What are the Four Last Things? Death, Judgment, Heaven, and Hell. Saint Philip Neri advised, "Beginners in religion ought to exercise themselves principally in meditation on the Four Last Things." And yet, more and more, we don't reflect on these things at all, make great efforts to avoid them in conversation, and rarely hear them mentioned by spiritual teachers.

We are only here on earth for the blink of an eye. This is not our home. That's why the happiness that God created us for is very different from the momentary pleasures of this world.

God created us for lasting happiness in this changing world and eternal joy with Him in Heaven forever. The happiness God desires for us in this life is a rare kind that is not dependent on situations or circumstances. It is easy to be happy when everything is going well. But Christian joy allows us to be happy even when we are suffering. This is one of the principal differences between Christianity and all other approaches to life.

Paul modeled this joy when he was in prison. From prison he wrote more about joy than any other topic. These writings are referred to as the "Prison Epistles" and include: Ephesians, Philippians, Colossians, and Philemon.

During his first imprisonment, which is mentioned in Acts 28, Paul wrote Ephesians to encourage the believers in Ephesus, and to explain the nature and the purpose of the Body of Christ—the Church. His letter to the Philippians teaches that true joy comes from Jesus Christ, and emphasizes the themes of Christian living: humility, personal sacrifice, and unity. Colossians teaches that Jesus is True God and True Man and the head of the Church. Philemon is a powerful teaching on Christian love and forgiveness. And throughout his writings, despite his trials and tribulations, the theme of joy shines through time and again. It is a joy fueled by his hope for Heaven—and not just for himself.

Do you ever think about Heaven? It seems to me we don't talk about it anywhere near as much as we should. When the famous English writer Rudyard Kipling was very ill a nurse asked him, "Is there anything you want?" He replied, "I want God!" We all do. We may not be aware of it, but we want God. Behind every desire for a car, handbag, watch, or a new house—is our desire for God. Behind every desire for a promotion, accomplishment, clothes and jewelry, plastic surgery, adventure and travel, food and sex, love, acceptance, and comfort—is our desire for God. We are always hungry for something more complete, and God is the completeness that we yearn for from the depths of our soul.

We are just passing through this world and it is helpful to remind ourselves of that from time to time. In the context of eternity, we are only here for the blink of an eye. Realizing this changes our priorities. At the same time, we are here for a reason, and God has a mission for you.

The phrase "live like you were dying" has become popular. But even in reflecting upon this concept, many people still manage to avoid the fundamental truth: We are dying. And for many people, living like you were dying has nothing to do with God or Heaven, and everything to do with the things of this world that separate us from God and Heaven.

But the reason the phrase "live like you were dying" has become so popular, the reason people need reminding, is because most people behave like they are going to live here on earth forever and as if there are no consequences for their actions. They won't and there are.

How many weeks of life does the average person get? Ask people to guess without calculating and they come up with some crazy answers. I asked a handful of people last week. One said 20,000. One said 50,000. One started calculating in his mind even though I had asked them not to do that.

But the truth: 4,000. If you are twenty, you have already had 1,000. If you're sixty, you're through 3,000 weeks. How many Sundays do you have left? Not many it turns out, even if you were born yesterday. So, don't waste a single Sunday. As my father used to say, "If you don't waste Sundays, you will be less likely to waste Mondays, Tuesdays, Wednesdays..."

How long do you think you will live? The average life span for an American is roughly eighty years. The uncomfortable reality is that from the moment we are born we are dying. Staying mindful of this inescapable truth leads us to live life to the fullest.

Which quarter of life are you in? If you are under twenty, you're still in the first quarter of life. Twenty-one to forty and you are in the second quarter, Forty-one to sixty is the third quarter, sixty-one to eighty is fourth quarter, and eighty-one or older means you are in extra time.

It is good for us to be mindful of death. It's not something to obsess about, but it is something to be aware of. This awareness provides perspective that allows us to assign correct value to the things and experiences of this world.

If you look around the world, so many of the problems are caused by assigning incorrect value to people, things, and experiences. And so many of our own problems are caused by over-valuing some things and undervaluing others. Of all the things, people, and experiences that we undervalue, the Eucharist is at the top of the list in all three categories.

If you knew you would die five years from today, what is it that you would make sure you did over the next five years? If today was your last day on this earth, what is it you wish you would have been more dedicated to?

Life is fleeting. In a moment we will all be gone. And what do you think comes next? Based on the teachings of Jesus Christ, the Catholic Church has always taught four things: Death, Judgment, Heaven, and Hell. Are you prepared to meet your Maker? And if you aren't, who and what can prepare you?

The Eucharist is the singular answer to the who and what of this question. Jesus in the Eucharist yearns to fill you with His Eucharistic Glory. If you allow Him to fill you with His glory, your ability to recognize truth, beauty, and goodness will increase; you will be filled with the grace necessary to endure life's inevitable challenges and unavoidable suffering; and His Eucharistic Glory will smooth the transition from this world to the next when that time comes.

"Live like you were dying." It's a brilliant idea. And of course, it means different things for different people depending on what you believe comes next. If you don't believe in God and you think this life is all there is, then this idea of living like you were dying is an invitation to recklessly indulge every hedonistic appetite imaginable. But if you believe in God and you trust what His Son Jesus shared with us during His time on earth, "live like you were dying" is a sobering reminder that life is short, eternity is long, and there are consequences to the way we choose to live our lives.

For a non-believer to "live like you were dying" leads to a life of colossal selfishness and devouring hopelessness. For a Christian to "live like you were dying" leads to a life of astounding love, rigorous discipline, heroic generosity, and an unconquerable hope. What do you believe comes next?

Trust. Surrender. Believe. Receive.

LESSON

Reflecting regularly on the Four Last Things—Death, Judgment, Heaven, and Hell—helps us to maintain perspective and live life to the fullest.

VIRTUE OF THE DAY

Faith: The virtue of faith is a gift. You can work hard to develop many virtues, but with faith, we ask: "Lord, increase my faith." Ask dozens of times each day. And as your faith grows, you will see more and more miracles, until finally, you will realize everything is a miracle.

SPIRITUAL COMMUNION

Jesus,
I believe that You are truly present
in the Most Holy Sacrament of the Eucharist.
Every day I long for more of You.
I love You above all things, and I desire to receive You into my soul.
Since I cannot receive You sacramentally at this moment,
I invite You to come and dwell in my heart.
May this spiritual communion increase my desire for the Eucharist.
You are the healer of my soul.
Take the blindness from my eyes,
the deafness from my ears,
the darkness from my mind,
and the hardness from my heart.

Fill me with the grace, wisdom, and courage to do Your will in all things.

My Lord and my God, draw me close to You, nearer than ever before. Amen.

THE PURPOSEFUL PILGRIM
DAY 4

"This is the day the Lord has made, let us rejoice and be glad."
Psalm 118:24

One of my favorite phrases in the New Testament is in Luke's Gospel. Jesus was making his way toward Jerusalem for Passover. The Jewish historian, Josephus, shares that on Passover the population of Jerusalem swelled to more than two million people and Jesus was among the pilgrims journeying toward the Holy City.

Scholars believe the first human settlements in Jerusalem date back to 3500 B.C. King David conquered the city and made it the capital of the Jewish kingdom around 1000 B.C. And his son Solomon built the first Temple in Jerusalem approximately forty years later.

So, Jewish pilgrimage to the Holy City began a millennium before the birth of Christ. Christians started journeying to Jerusalem in the first century. And Muslims began their pilgrimages to Jerusalem in the seventh century, following the death of Muhammad.

This makes Jerusalem a converging holy site for all three of the world's major monotheistic religions: Christianity, Judaism, and Islam.

In the ninth chapter of Luke's Gospel, we read about Jesus on pilgrimage to Jerusalem: "Now it happened that as the time drew near for Him to be taken up to Heaven, He resolutely turned His face towards Jerusalem (Luke 9:51)."

He didn't just go, He went *resolutely*.

Some translations use. . .

"He *resolutely determined* to journey to Jerusalem."

"He *steadfastly set His face* to go to Jerusalem."

"He *steadfastly and determinedly* set His face to go to Jerusalem."

Others add... *"to fulfill His purpose."*

What do we approach with the same passion and commitment, determination and steadfastness as Jesus approached Jerusalem? Anything? Probably not. And what does that say about us?

Some people will convince themselves that they should be more committed to some worldly pursuit. But the truth is, the reason we have not committed ourselves so fully, so totally, so completely to anything in this world, is that we are made for more. This type of commitment belongs to God and to God alone.

We are called to pursue Heaven, which is union with God, with that kind of steadfastness, determination, focus, and clarity. We are called to pursue Heaven as resolutely as Jesus determined to journey toward His death and resurrection in Jerusalem.

Jesus set off toward Jerusalem with determined resolve. It is time to bring that focus and clarity to our lives.

Every encounter with Jesus in the Eucharist, whether it is at Mass on Sunday or sitting before the tabernacle for a few moments in an empty church, increases our clarity about what matters most and what doesn't matter at all. Most people are confused about what really matters, and God wants to liberate us from that confusion.

Eucharistic clarity leads us to focus on the right things. We all get to choose who and what we care about, and who and what we choose to care about determines everything. For whatever we focus on will increase in our lives.

Catholics are not called to wander aimlessly through life. There are too many people tragically wandering aimlessly through life. There have been times when you and I have lived our lives that way, wandering aimlessly and indulging every manner of distraction. But now it is time to quit the endless wandering and take on the determination of a purposeful pilgrim. That is exactly what we are striving to do as we prepare for Eucharistic Consecration.

Jesus resolutely determined to journey to Jerusalem. Let's apply that resolute determination to our earthly pilgrimage toward the Eternal City. Are you determined?

Trust. Surrender. Believe. Receive.

LESSON
A purposeful pilgrim sets aside the distractions of this world and is resolutely determined to journey to Heaven.

VIRTUE OF THE DAY
Determination: The virtue of determination allows us to focus on a task and see it through to completion. Just keep moving in the direction of your goal or destination. Determination is taking the next step, no matter how small that step may be.

SPIRITUAL COMMUNION
Jesus,
I believe that You are truly present
in the Most Holy Sacrament of the Eucharist.
Every day I long for more of You.
I love You above all things, and I desire to receive You into my soul.
Since I cannot receive You sacramentally at this moment,
I invite You to come and dwell in my heart.
May this spiritual communion increase my desire for the Eucharist.
You are the healer of my soul.
Take the blindness from my eyes,
the deafness from my ears,
the darkness from my mind,
and the hardness from my heart.

Fill me with the grace, wisdom, and courage to do Your will in all things.

My Lord and my God, draw me close to You, nearer than ever before.

Amen.

FEAR OF MISSING OUT
DAY 5

"This is the day the Lord has made, let us rejoice and be glad."
Psalm 118:24

Without the purposeful determination of a pilgrim, we are destined to live a life of distraction.

One hundred and fifty years ago, Henry David Thoreau left Concord, Massachusetts, because he believed it had become too noisy, too busy, too distracting. He went out to Walden Pond to reconnect with himself and with nature. It took him only seven pages in his writings to conclude that, "Most men lead lives of quiet desperation."

Today, most men and women lead lives of distraction. Lack of focus leads to lack of commitment, and together these lead us to lives of quiet (and not so quiet) desperation.

Consecration changes all of that. It challenges us to name what matters most. It gives us the clarity and wisdom to focus on the vital few rather than chasing the trivial many. It encourages us to place Jesus at the center of our days and weeks. And it liberates us from all the distraction and superficiality that dominates the culture.

I had a college roommate who was constantly running from one thing to the next, sacrificing sleep, and neglecting schoolwork. One day I asked him why he was choosing this path and he said to me, "I don't want to miss out on anything during these four years." This state has come to be known as FOMO—Fear of Missing Out.

The idea that if we make the right choices, squeeze enough into each day, and become ultra-efficient, we won't miss out on things is a colossal error. More than an error, it is a delusion. You are going to miss out. In fact, you are certain to miss out on the great majority of things, experiences, and opportunities.

One of the biggest traps a pilgrim can fall into is the trap of FOMO. Driven by the psychological nonsense of FOMO, many people make the worst decisions of their lives.

FOMO also has a close cousin known as "settling." The accepted wisdom of the vast universe known as the Internet is that you should never settle. This is horrible advice. The two most common expressions of this nonsense relate to relationships and career. "Settling" romantically means committing to someone who is less than ideal for you. The professional version of this nonsense involves "settling" for a job that pays the bills and supports your family rather than pursuing your dreams.

The truth is this: you have to settle. You don't have a choice. It is unavoidable. Our lives are finite. You do not have infinite time on this earth to pursue all possibilities. Your time is limited. You cannot become successful at anything without first settling on that path. To become a successful teacher or doctor, you set aside the possibilities of other careers and commit yourself to being a teacher or a doctor. If you bounce from one career to the next, never mastering any particular craft, you are "settling" in a different, much more diabolical way.

One of the main reasons so many young people are increasingly having trouble maintaining significant romantic relationships is because they want to keep all their options open. But keeping all your options open shuts down the possibility of success in the one relationship you are in at this moment.

Every decision is a decision to miss out. Every choice for something is a choice to miss out on everything else.

FOMO and "settling" both foster unrealistic ideals that nobody can live up to due to the innate limitations of life and all human beings. The result is a growing anxiety because we are constantly missing out and settling is inevitable.

Consecrating ourselves to Jesus in the Eucharist changes all this. We are no longer afraid of missing out. We know it is preferable to miss out on most things, because the only things that really matter are those that God has in mind just for you. Doing the will of God, therefore, transforms FOMO into JOMO—the Joy of Missing Out.

We each have to decide for ourselves if we are going to lead a life of distraction or a life of focus.

The world promotes a shallow and superficial path, but this path doesn't lead anywhere worth going. I love what Willy Wonka says, "A little nonsense now and then is treasured by the wisest men." Lightheartedness is a wonderful thing. Humor is gift from God. But life is a serious thing. It should be taken seriously. Humor and lightheartedness are designed to help us carry the serious burden of life—not to avoid seriousness altogether.

The world tells people, "You think too much." What a horrible message. The world tells people, "Relax. Enjoy yourself." These are important, but when all you do is relax and enjoy yourself, chances are you are headed down a long, cold, dark, lonely road.

This road leads to comfort addiction. A couple of weeks ago, I was speaking with a friend, and he said something that made me stop and reflect: "Everybody is looking for an easier, softer way." It's a generalization. It may not be true for everyone. But it sure seems true for most people. We want life to be easier. We want the path we walk to be softer. We want to be comfortable.

Is comfort good for us? Is the comfortable path the way of the Christian? It seems that it isn't. This is not simply my opinion. There may be many things that seem unclear when we read the Gospels, but the general criteria for following Jesus is abundantly clear. In Matthew's Gospel we read, "If anyone wishes to come after me, let him deny himself and take up his cross, and follow me." (Matthew 16:24) Deny yourself. Jesus was clear. He didn't promise or even allude to an easy path. He did not promise comfort. He promised quite the opposite. He set denial of self as a primary condition of discipleship, and He promised that each of us would have a cross of our own to carry.

Why doesn't Jesus want us to get comfortable? The reason is simple, profound, and practical: He doesn't want us to forget that we are just passing through this world. We are pilgrims. When we get comfortable, we start to behave as if we are going to live on this earth forever—and we are not.

Perhaps if our lives have become comfortable, that alone is a sign that we have wandered away from the Gospel path. When was the last time you denied yourself? Was it a large or small thing?

Consecrating yourself and your life to Jesus in the Eucharist is a serious thing. It will be uncomfortable at times, but it will also bring you spiritual gratification like none you have ever known before now.

A little seriousness is deeply agreeable to the human spirit. Deep thought is good for us. The modern obsession with comfort is an aversion to depth and seriousness, and it exiles too many people from God, religion, spirituality, the Church, dynamic relationships, healthy parenting, rigorous careers, and so much more.

Jesus comforted people in their afflictions and afflicted people in their comfort. The saints did the same thing. If you sit in the presence of Jesus in the Eucharist, you can expect the same. He longs to comfort you in your afflictions and afflict you in your comfort.

Trust. Surrender. Believe. Receive.

LESSON

One of the biggest traps a pilgrim can fall into is the trap of FOMO.

Driven by the psychological nonsense of FOMO, many people make the worst decisions of their lives. The only things that matter are those that God has chosen for you. It is preferable to miss out on everything else. Doing the will of God transforms FOMO into JOMO—the Joy of Missing Out.

VIRTUE OF THE DAY

Discipline: The virtue of discipline allows us to maximize our contribution to the world. Joy is a byproduct of realizing our God-given potential. You will never have more joy than discipline. By choosing to discipline ourselves, we suffer less and cause less suffering for others.

SPIRITUAL COMMUNION

Jesus,
I believe that You are truly present
in the Most Holy Sacrament of the Eucharist.
Every day I long for more of You.
I love You above all things, and I desire to receive You into my soul.
Since I cannot receive You sacramentally at this moment,
I invite You to come and dwell in my heart.
May this spiritual communion increase my desire for the Eucharist.
You are the healer of my soul.
Take the blindness from my eyes,
the deafness from my ears,
the darkness from my mind,
and the hardness from my heart.
Fill me with the grace, wisdom, and courage to do Your will in all things.
My Lord and my God, draw me close to You, nearer than ever before.
Amen.

SIX DEFINING SPIRITUAL MOMENTS
DAY 6

"This is the day the Lord has made, let us rejoice and be glad."
Psalm 118:24

The spiritual life is chief among serious endeavors. Something that is serious is demanding and requires careful consideration and earnest application. Our need for depth and seriousness is best met with a rich inner life.

The spiritual life is made up of seasons, and even in the darkest moments it is important to remind ourselves that spring will come again. What is unchanging allows us to make sense of change. The six lessons I am about to share with you have served me well in every season.

Over the past thirty-five years, I have experienced many seasons in my spiritual life: long stretches of great spiritual consistency; other stretches when I have been inconsistent in my prayer; times of resistance and times of surrender; seasons of great patience and seasons of selfish impatience; periods when I couldn't wait to get to prayer and periods when I had to force myself to keep showing up; days when I felt the warmth of God's love fill my whole being and days when I felt so cold it seemed He could not be further away from me; weeks when I felt I was in the thickest fog and months when I saw things with great clarity; seasons of trial when nothing seemed to go right and seasons of triumph when it seemed nothing could go wrong.

The six lessons I am about to describe to you had a seismic impact on my inner and outer life, and I am confident they will also have a great impact on your life. The definition of seismic is "of enormous proportions or effect"; I use that word very deliberately here.

The First Shift: Just Begin the Conversation. This is the first seismic shift in the spiritual life. Prayer is a conversation. Once the conversation has begun, it can lead anywhere. Most important, it will lead to the places it needs to lead to. Never underestimate how important it is to just begin the conversation. This is true with your friends and colleagues, your brothers and sisters, your spouse and children, and of course with God.

This first shift requires us to make the journey from the head to the heart, to turn from a thinking type of prayer to a relational style of prayer. It is about learning to pray from your heart.

The Second Shift: Ask God What He Wants. The second of these seismic shifts occurs within the conversation when we stop asking God for what we want and start asking what He wants.

The majority of prayers mumbled and muttered, whispered and screamed on the planet today will be asking God for something. This second shift is seismic because it is when we begin to ask the Big Question: "God, what do You think I should do?"

When we start asking God for advice, direction, inspiration, and guidance, this is a significant moment. When we stop asking Him for things, for favors, and for our will to be done, we begin to open ourselves to much more than His will. We open ourselves to His wisdom. As we mature spiritually, we realize that to want anything other than the will of God is foolish and futile. But in the early stages of our spiritual development, the will of God can seem heavy, restrictive, and burdensome, even though the opposite is true.

The other thing that happens when we ask God about His ways and plans is that we begin to adopt a spiritual curiosity. This curiosity about God and His dreams for us and the world can be incredibly invigorating. It transforms the way we see ourselves, other people, creation, society, and indeed God Himself.

Getting what we want doesn't make us happy. We know that

from experience. The wise seek the will of God in all things.

The Third Shift: Give Yourself to Prayer. The third seismic shift that occurs in the inner life is when we stop doing our prayer and start giving ourselves to prayer.

Giving yourself to prayer means showing up and letting God do what He wants to do with you during that time of prayer. It means letting go of expectations and agendas for our time with God. It means detachment from the feelings that prayer provokes within us.

In *The Seven Levels of Intimacy,* I introduced the concept of *carefree timelessness.* Carefree timelessness is the reason young people fall in love so easily, and the lack of carefree timelessness is the reason so many couples fall out of love. What is carefree timelessness? Time together without an agenda.

The third seismic shift of the spiritual life requires us to surrender to the experience and to believe that God is working in us even when it feels like we are not accomplishing anything. It is about enjoying some carefree timelessness with God.

What makes it difficult is that so much of our lives are focused on doing and accomplishing. This shift requires us to let go and focus on being. The shift from doing prayer to giving ourselves to prayer may seem subtle, but the reality is it is one of the most significant inner changes that can take place in our souls.

The Fourth Shift: Transform Everything into Prayer. Prayer is not an activity that encompasses a small portion of our days. It is a way of life. Prayer awakens our spiritual senses and we become aware of God at our side throughout the day. Not that He is in our presence, but that we are continually in His presence.

The fourth seismic shift occurs when we discover that every activity can be transformed into prayer by offering it to God. "Pray constantly," was Saint Paul's invitation, and it is a beautiful spiritual principle.

Learning to transform daily activities into prayer was one of the greatest spiritual lessons of my life. Offer the next hour of your work for a friend who is sick. Offer the task you are least looking forward to today to God as a prayer for the person you know who is suffering most today, and do that task with great love, better than you have ever done it. Offer each task, one at a time, to God as a prayer for a specific intention, and do so with love.

The Fifth Shift: Make Yourself Available. Do you wish to know the secret to supreme happiness? Strip away everything in your heart that makes you less available to God. The joy we experience is proportional to how available we make ourselves to God.

The fifth shift is about making ourselves 100 percent available to God. Consecration is ultimately about making ourselves available to God. Prayer is about making ourselves available to God.

Through prayer, our spiritual awareness is constantly fine-tuned, and the more fine-tuned it becomes, the more we come to see that so few things really matter. The challenge, then, is to focus on the things that really matter. Is your life focused on the things that matter most?

The fifth seismic shift in the spiritual life is availability. It is about surrendering ourselves, our plan, and our lives to God. It is through this surrender that our ultimate transformation takes place. It is through this surrender that we make ourselves 100 percent available to God, allowing Him to transform us and our lives.

How available are you to God? Are you ready to surrender and make yourself completely available to Him?

The Sixth Shift: Just Keep Showing Up. No matter what, just keep showing up to prayer. Keep showing up to Mass. Keep showing up for your spiritual routines and rituals. We will explore this sixth shift in more detail tomorrow, but for now, it's enough to be mindful that it's not about what we are doing. It's about what God is doing in us, through us, and with us—when we show up.

It is important to remember that God does all the heavy lifting in the spiritual life. The six seismic shifts are things that God does in us. All He asks is that we open ourselves to Him and cooperate. If we start feeling overwhelmed spiritually, there is a fairly good chance that we have confused our role with God's role.

The Eucharist floods our souls with the grace needed to respond to these six seismic shifts with courage and wisdom. Each time we receive Jesus in the Eucharist, spend time in the presence of the Eucharist, or acknowledge Jesus' presence in a tabernacle, our souls flood with grace.

Consecrating yourself to Jesus in the Eucharist involves all six of these spiritual shifts. We will eventually arrive at these six significant moments in the spiritual life organically if we stay committed to the journey. This consecration process will raise our awareness of them all over these thirty-three days.

Trust. Surrender. Believe. Receive.

LESSON

The spiritual life is not about what we are doing. It's about what God is doing in us, through us, and with us—when we surrender and make ourselves available to Him.

VIRTUE OF THE DAY

Surrender: The virtue of surrender leads to tranquility. If you find yourself wrestling with every situation or doing battle with every person, it's time to explore why you are so insistent on imposing your will on every person and situation. The secret to surrendering to God is knowing your responsibilities and being clear about His responsibilities. Our willingness to surrender says a lot about our understanding of God.

SPIRITUAL COMMUNION

Jesus,

I believe that You are truly present

in the Most Holy Sacrament of the Eucharist.

Every day I long for more of You.

I love You above all things, and I desire to receive You into my soul.

Since I cannot receive You sacramentally at this moment,

I invite You to come and dwell in my heart.

May this spiritual communion increase my desire for the Eucharist.

You are the healer of my soul.

Take the blindness from my eyes,

the deafness from my ears,

the darkness from my mind,

and the hardness from my heart.

Fill me with the grace, wisdom, and courage to do Your will in all things.

My Lord and my God, draw me close to You, nearer than ever before.

Amen.

THE PILGRIM'S VIRTUE
DAY 7

"This is the day the Lord has made, let us rejoice and be glad."
Psalm 118:24

By the second Friday of January most New Year's resolutions have been abandoned. On this seventh day of our thirty-three-day journey together, I want to encourage you to persevere. Perseverance is the pilgrim's virtue. Many people will abandon this path of consecration. Decide that you will not be one of them.

The most practical wisdom I have ever received about prayer was from an old priest many years ago, when I was a teenager and first starting to take my spiritual life seriously. The initial excitement had worn off and I was experiencing the early signs of dryness and desolation in prayer. Our natural and very human reaction when prayer doesn't "feel good" is to wonder what we are doing wrong. Prayer should never be judged by how it makes us feel, and we often aren't doing anything wrong. Prayer isn't about feelings.

"Just keep showing up," the old priest said to me. I didn't understand at first and when I asked him what he meant, he replied, "I'm speaking plainly. No hidden meanings, boy. Just keep showing up. Show up each day regardless of how you feel or if it is convenient. Just show up and let God work on you."

This is the sixth seismic shift we mentioned yesterday. It occurs when showing up for our daily prayer is no longer a daily decision. It becomes a commitment, a decision that no matter what you are going to show up and be with God for that time each day.

The only failure in prayer is to stop praying. You will think and feel things, and many of them don't mean what you initially think they do. So, keep showing up. Sit with whatever it is that God says to you and reveals to you. Just keep showing up.

Some days prayer will seem easy and others it will seem difficult. How it seems is never a good indication of how fruitful prayer is. Try not to judge your prayer. It is foolish to say, "I prayed well today." It takes at least ten years to determine whether you prayed well today. Just keep showing up.

If God gives you the grace of encouragement and inspiration, fabulous. Accept it, embrace it, don't squander it, put it to good use. But if you come away from prayer discouraged on some days, remember that Jesus died on the Cross and that was an immense victory. And yet, don't see that as an invitation to a life of misery that you design for yourself by creating crosses that God never intended you to carry. Life will bring you enough suffering and challenges without you needing to look for more. Just keep showing up and God will teach you all these things and so many others.

For myself, though there have been times when prayer has seemed effortless, for the most part it doesn't come particularly easily. There are days when I have more enthusiasm for it than others. And there are days when it is difficult, even excruciating. These days require me to force myself to be present despite these struggles. And of course, there are days when it's wonderful and blissful. It all just depends on what God is doing.

In your spiritual life there will be long and dusty roads, epic mountaintop experiences, moments of fear and trembling in the dark valleys, beautiful mornings filled with hope, and long dark nights drenched with hopelessness. Throughout your journey you will need an ever-flowing stream of practical insights to help you take the next step, but none will serve you better than the simple wisdom of that old priest, "Just keep showing up!"

No matter what, just keep showing up. Remember, it is not about what we are doing. It's about what God is doing in us, through us, and with us—when we show up.

Nowhere is this advice more relevant than when it comes to the Eucharist. Imagine if Catholics had applied this simple wisdom to the practice of attending Mass over the past fifty years: *Just keep showing up. Show up each Sunday regardless of how you feel or if it is convenient. Just show up and let God work on you.* Imagine. The Catholic Church and the state of society would be completely different today if we had just kept showing up and letting God work.

The counsel of Blessed Pier Giorgio Frassati is more needed today than ever before, because so many people have abandoned Sunday Mass: "With all the strength of my soul I urge you to approach the Communion table as often as you can. Feed on this bread of angels and you will draw all the energy you need to fight inner battles. Because true happiness, dear friends, does not consist in the pleasures of the world or in earthly things, but in peace of conscience, which we have only if we are pure in heart and mind."

Never forget that each time you receive Jesus in the Eucharist He is working in you, to send you out into the world so that He can work through you.

Trust. Surrender. Believe. Receive.

LESSON

Just keep showing up for prayer and your other spiritual practices. Show up each day regardless of how you feel, or if it is convenient, or whether or not you think it is bearing any fruit. God's ways are mysterious. He is at work in your soul like the roots of a mighty tree beneath the surface. Just because you don't know what God is doing doesn't mean He isn't preparing you for whatever is next. Just show up and let Him work on you.

VIRTUE OF THE DAY

Perseverance: The virtue of perseverance is essential for friendship and love. Perseverance teaches us to resolve difficulties. Acquiring this virtue requires both grace and significant personal effort. There is no virtue in beginning. It is easy. Many start, few finish. This is true in almost everything. Don't look at how far you still have to go, look at how far you have come, and consider how your life would be if you had never found this path at all.

SPIRITUAL COMMUNION

Jesus,
I believe that You are truly present
in the Most Holy Sacrament of the Eucharist.
Every day I long for more of You.
I love You above all things, and I desire to receive You into my soul.
Since I cannot receive You sacramentally at this moment,
I invite You to come and dwell in my heart.
May this spiritual communion increase my desire for the Eucharist.
You are the healer of my soul.
Take the blindness from my eyes,
the deafness from my ears,
the darkness from my mind,
and the hardness from my heart.
Fill me with the grace, wisdom, and courage to do Your will in all things.
My Lord and my God, draw me close to You, nearer than ever before.
Amen.

WEEK TWO

The Eucharist
and the
Saints

MOTHER TERESA: SPIRITUAL HABITS DAY 8

"Set your minds on the things that are above, not on earthly things."
Colossians 3:2

Mother Teresa is one of the most beloved women of all time. She emerged as an icon of goodness in the modern world. Capturing the imagination of the whole world with her heroic acts of service for "the poorest of poor," she was a steadfast voice of faith and love in a world gone mad with materialism and hedonism. Contrasted against the unbridled materialism of the modern world, the simplicity of her life caused men and women in all states in life to reflect upon the way they were choosing to live their own lives. At a time when secularism had a firm grip on the soul of our culture, her humility could hold the attention of any crowd as she spoke profound spiritual truths. This Catholic nun intrigued the hearts, confounded the minds, and inspired the spirits of people of every faith and nation. With no product to sell and no public relations representatives, she became one of most famous people in the world. And her mere presence was so magnetic and powerful that world leaders and celebrities of every type were often left baffled. Her appeal was truly Catholic—universal. She was truly a remarkable woman.

Her faith wasn't a speech, it was living and breathing. She saw each moment as an opportunity to love. Every individual person mattered to her. "I believe in person-to-person contact," she once said, "every person is Christ for me, and since there is only one Jesus, the person I am meeting is the one person in the world at that moment."

Those who spent time with her would often comment, "For the moment you were with her, there was only you and her. She wasn't looking over your shoulder to see what was happening around you. You had her full attention. It was as if nothing else existed to her except you."

Mother Teresa was considered a living saint for decades during her lifetime and was canonized on September 4, 2016, just nineteen years after her death.

What makes the saints different from the billions of other people throughout history? What sets them apart? Their habits. The things they did with unerring consistency every day, week, month, and year.

Make an inventory of the habits that define the lives of the saints, and it is a fairly short list. What are the things they did each day, week, month, year? Simple things like the habit of daily prayer and an annual retreat, praying the rosary and caring for the poor. And the overlap from one saint to another is massive. They didn't all have vastly different habits, but remarkably similar habits.

This is why it is a mistake to go looking for new and different ways to the spiritual life. This type of quest is usually driven by the ego and fueled by pride, and therefore, lacks the essential ingredient for spiritual growth: humility.

The path of Christian spiritualty is well trodden. It is not a secret or a mystery, it is easy to discover and available to anyone, and it works.

When I reflect on the life of Mother Teresa, the questions I ask myself are: Where did her power to love so deeply come from? What was the source of her strength to serve so selflessly? How was this woman able to inspire so many people to give their lives to God?

The answers to these questions are also deeply embedded in her life. Before everything else, Mother Teresa was a woman of prayer. Each day, for decades, she spent time in prayer before the Blessed Sacrament. Her power to love, her strength to endure, and her gift to inspire others were all born from the Eucharist. This woman believed in the centrality of Jesus Christ. She knew His centrality in history and eternity, and she trusted His centrality in her own life. There is the source: Jesus in the Eucharist. She placed Jesus at the center of her life.

Eucharistic Adoration was one of Mother Teresa's primary spiritual habits. Spending time with Jesus in the Eucharist was an essential part of what made her who she was. It is a habit she shared with almost every saint who has ever lived. The world was obsessed with the power and magnetism of her goodness, and yet, the world ignored the source of the holiness she manifested everywhere she went.

It would have been easy for her to lose herself in the enormous fame the world lavished on her. Why didn't she? The media is full of stories about famous people who have been chewed up and spat out by fame. Why didn't fame affect Mother Teresa in the same way?

She spent the first hour of each day before the Blessed Sacrament in Adoration. As the impact of her work grew, some of those close to her asked her to reduce this to thirty minutes, pointing out that every minute she spent with people bore tremendous fruit. This may have seemed reasonable and rational to those proposing the change, especially in light of all of Mother Teresa's other daily spiritual practices. So, did she capitulate? No. She increased her time of Adoration to two hours each morning and reminded those closest to her that Jesus was the source of all the fruit their work was bearing. Later, as her legend grew, she increased her daily Adoration to three hours.

Our lives change when our habits change. What problem are you trying to solve in your life right now? Do you see how the habit of Adoration would help you solve that problem? Do you see how the habit of Adoration would have helped you avoid that problem to begin with?

How would your life change if you spent an hour each day before the Blessed Sacrament? Try not to dismiss the question. I realize that for most people this is not possible, but consider it for a moment anyway. How would your life change? Get lost in that reflection for a few moments. Think on it as you go about your day.

Now, consider this. What is possible? One hour a week? One hour each month? Ten minutes each day? Because whatever is possible, you should grasp it and allow the power of the Eucharist to pour into your soul.

Follow Mother Teresa's advice, "If I can give you any advice, I beg you to get closer to the Eucharist and to Jesus. . . We must pray to Jesus to give us that tenderness of the Eucharist."

The French novelist, Léon Bloy, once wrote, "The only real sadness, the only real failure, the only great tragedy in life, is not to become a saint." While becoming a saint is the primary goal of the Christian life, most people never seriously consider it a possibility. Is it possible? Yes. How do we begin? By adopting the spiritual habits that the saints shared in common.

You need the habit of Adoration. How often? I don't know. For how long? I don't know. That is between you and God, but it was central to the lives of the saints, and I encourage you to make it central to your life even if it is only for one hour each month.

It has been observed that people emulate the five people they spend most time with—for better or worse. Make Jesus one of those five people. Spending time in the presence of Jesus in the Eucharist will transform you and your life in ways you cannot even begin to imagine.

Trust. Surrender. Believe. Receive.

LESSON

Our lives change when our habits change. Adopting the habit of Eucharistic Adoration will change every aspect of your life. We tend to emulate the people we spend time with. By spending time in the presence of Jesus in the Eucharist, we become more like Him.

VIRTUE OF THE DAY

Consistency: The virtue of consistency allows us to moderate our behavior in alignment with our faith and values. It demands that we abandon frivolous whims, preferences, and cravings as they arise throughout the day and stay true to the course we have set. It also requires constant micro-alignments between your words, beliefs, and actions. A consistent man conducts himself and corrects himself in order to maintain his true north bearing. A woman with the virtue of consistency is a great comfort to her friends and family. Consistent people are sometimes mistaken for being boring, but only by those who don't value the rare peace consistency ushers quietly into our lives.

SPIRITUAL COMMUNION

Jesus,
I believe that You are truly present
in the Most Holy Sacrament of the Eucharist.
Every day I long for more of You.
I love You above all things, and I desire to receive You into my soul.
Since I cannot receive You sacramentally at this moment,
I invite You to come and dwell in my heart.
May this spiritual communion increase my desire for the Eucharist.
You are the healer of my soul.
Take the blindness from my eyes,
the deafness from my ears,
the darkness from my mind,

and the hardness from my heart.

Fill me with the grace, wisdom, and courage to do Your will in all things.

My Lord and my God, draw me close to You, nearer than ever before. Amen.

JOHN PAUL II:
PRAYER AFTER COMMUNION
DAY 9

"Set your minds on the things that are above, not on earthly things."
Colossians 3:2

One prayer after communion changed my life. I was thirteen years old and Pope John Paul II was visiting Australia. My father took me to an enormous outdoor Mass. It wasn't my prayer that changed my life, it was John Paul II's prayer. His witness. His example.

Did you ever see Pope John Paul II pray? Each morning, he celebrated Mass in his private chapel with about twenty guests. Perhaps you know someone who was fortunate enough to attend. Or perhaps you saw television footage of one of those Masses.

When this man knelt down to pray after Communion, he would close his eyes and go to a place deep within himself. Once he was there, nothing and no one could distract him from communing with God. What does it mean to commune with God? To share your intimate thoughts and feelings. Pope John Paul II would go to that place deep within himself, and from that place he brought forth the fruit of his life: wisdom, compassion, generosity, understanding, patience, courage, insight, forgiveness, humility, inspiration, and a love so apparent you could almost touch it.

In those moments after Communion, he allowed nothing to distract him from his prayer. He let nothing draw his attention away from his Divine Visitor in those precious moments after receiving the Blessed Sacrament.

The amazing thing is, if you put the same man in a football stadium with a hundred thousand people and a million more distractions, he would still kneel down after Communion, close his eyes, and go to that place deep within him where he connected with God. And he lived his life from that place.

Find that place within you. Find that place deep, deep within yourself, the place where you can connect with God and your truest self. If you do nothing else with your life, find that place, spend more and more time in that place, and begin to live your life from that deep place.

How do you find the deep place within you? There is one way that I can guarantee will work. Befriend silence. I am not suggesting that you spend four, five, six hours a day in silence. Drop by a church during the day when it is empty and quiet. Find a quiet corner and a comfortable chair at home. Leave the music off in the car on the way to work. Have a television-free evening once a week. Try it. It works. If you want to live from the deep place within you, visit the classroom of silence each day for a few minutes.

Pope John Paul II wrote, "The Eucharist is the secret of my day. It gives strength and meaning to all my activities of service to the Church and to the whole world... Let Jesus in the Blessed Sacrament speak to your hearts. It is He who is the true answer of life that you seek. He stays here with us: He is God with us. Seek Him without tiring, welcome Him without reserve, love Him without interruption: today, tomorrow, forever."

What is the secret to your day?

Trust. Surrender. Believe. Receive.

LESSON

Befriend silence, so as to find and spend time in that place deep within, where you are able to connect with your truest self and God. The more time you spend in silence, the more you will be able to live your life from that deep place.

VIRTUE OF THE DAY

Attentiveness: The virtue of attentiveness is a sign of care for others and care for the soul, which is an immeasurable gift from God. Attentive people notice things, inside themselves, in the situations and circumstances of daily life, and in other people. They notice the person in the room who is suffering the most. Sustained attention in prayer is developed by practicing sustained attention in our work and with other people. Give the person in front of you in each moment your full attention.

SPIRITUAL COMMUNION

Jesus,

I believe that You are truly present
in the Most Holy Sacrament of the Eucharist.
Every day I long for more of You.
I love You above all things, and I desire to receive You into my soul.
Since I cannot receive You sacramentally at this moment,
I invite You to come and dwell in my heart.
May this spiritual communion increase my desire for the Eucharist.
You are the healer of my soul.
Take the blindness from my eyes,
the deafness from my ears,
the darkness from my mind,
and the hardness from my heart.
Fill me with the grace, wisdom, and courage to do Your will in all things.
My Lord and my God, draw me close to You, nearer than ever before.
Amen.

THÉRÈSE OF LISIEUX:
JESUS IN EVERY TABERNACLE
DAY 10

"Set your minds on the things that are above, not on earthly things."
Colossians 3:2

A couple of days ago we explored a little of Mother Teresa's remarkable story, but the story within the story is equally remarkable. Have you ever wondered how Mother Teresa learned to live, love, and pray the way she did?

This question leads us to another amazing Catholic woman that Mother Teresa never met, another nun who lived in a Carmelite convent in southern France. Her name was Saint Thérèse of Lisieux. Thérèse believed that love is expressed through attention to the small things that fill our daily lives. Mother Teresa practiced "The Little Way" taught by Thérèse, and shared "The Little Way" with millions of people around the world.

This connection demonstrates that every Holy Moment is a historic event. Every time we choose to love God, and collaborate with Him to love our neighbor, we change the course of human history, because our Holy Moments reverberate powerfully in the lives of people in other places and other times.

Thérèse of Lisieux entered the convent at the age of fifteen and died at age twenty-four, but her influence continues to resonate in the lives of more than 4,500 Missionaries of Charity (the order Mother Teresa founded) who work in 133 countries today. It is impossible to measure Saint Thérèse of Lisieux's impact on history, but it is vast. Holiness is deeply personal, but it is also communal and historic. Holiness is not something we do for ourselves; it is something God does in us when we cooperate. It is something He does in us, not for us alone, but for others and for all of history.

Thérèse of Lisieux was a great teacher for Mother Teresa, and she will generously share her wisdom with us if we open ourselves to "The Little Way."

We live in a world that worships complexity and grandiosity, but the genius of God is found in the simplicity of ordinary things. The Eucharist is the ultimate expression of His ordinary way, coming to us in the simplicity of bread and wine.

Thérèse of Lisieux is one of the most popular and influential saints in the history of the Catholic Church. Pope Pius X called her "the greatest saint of modern times." Known for her love of the ordinary way, the simple way, "The Little Way," she championed a spiritualty that is accessible to people of all ages, regardless of intellectual formation or vocation in life.

Her approach to the spiritual life was simple and practical. And this model of holiness is as powerful today as ever before.

I will offer you *the simplest way* I know to adopt it: Be mindful of God's presence in each moment of each day. How? I will offer you the most practical way I know. At every moment, of every day, for the rest of your life, know where the nearest tabernacle is.

Where is the nearest tabernacle to your home? How close is the nearest tabernacle to your workplace? When you go on vacation, find out where the nearest tabernacle is. Where is Jesus? In the nearest tabernacle.

"Do you realize that Jesus is there in the tabernacle expressly for you? He burns with the desire to come into your heart." These are the words of Saint Thérèse of Lisieux.

She learned to live with God in the present moment. "If I did not simply live from one moment to another, it would be impossible for me to be patient, but I only look at the present, I forget the past, and I take good care not to forestall the future."

She understood God's love of simplicity. "Our Lord does not look so much at the greatness of our actions, or even at their difficulty, as at the love with which we do them."

Little things done with great love. This is what we are called to. The small things. The simple things. The practical things.

Our egos worship the complexity and grandiosity, but it is the little things that lead to great love. It is the simple things that lead our souls to flourish.

Trust. Surrender. Believe. Receive.

LESSON
Always be mindful of God's presence in the world. Where is the nearest tabernacle? At every moment, of every day, for the rest of your life, know the answer to this question.

VIRTUE OF THE DAY
Spiritual Awareness: The virtue of spiritual awareness is marked by a sensitivity to the presence of God. It makes us mindful of how different people, things, and experiences unite us with God or draw us away from Him.

SPIRITUAL COMMUNION
Jesus,
I believe that You are truly present
in the Most Holy Sacrament of the Eucharist.
Every day I long for more of You.
I love You above all things, and I desire to receive You into my soul.
Since I cannot receive You sacramentally at this moment,
I invite You to come and dwell in my heart.
May this spiritual communion increase my desire for the Eucharist.
You are the healer of my soul.
Take the blindness from my eyes,

the deafness from my ears,
the darkness from my mind,
and the hardness from my heart.
Fill me with the grace, wisdom, and courage to do Your will in all things.
My Lord and my God, draw me close to You, nearer than ever before.
Amen.

MAXIMILIAN KOLBE: NO LOVE WITHOUT SACRIFICE DAY 11

"Set your minds on the things that are above, not on earthly things."
Colossians 3:2

Our love of comfort eliminates sacrifice from our lives, and there is no love without sacrifice, so our obsession with comfort is eliminating love.

In a world that can be cold and harsh, violent and at times brutal, the saints prove that our humanity has a better side. Our better side is kind and caring, compassionate and gentle. The saints fostered this better side with spiritual disciplines and acts of loving service. These acts required personal sacrifices that can be directly linked to the Cross via the Eucharist.

Maximilian Kolbe demonstrated the power of love and sacrifice in the midst of the brutality of Nazi Germany. His moment of heroic selflessness was an epic demonstration of generosity. In the face of cold indifference, it was a moment of white-hot glowing love. In the face of stunning brutality, it was a moment of gentle surrender.

Kolbe was a priest in Poland during World War II. After Germany invaded Poland he organized a temporary hospital in the monastery where he lived, with the help of a few brothers who remained. Between 1939 and 1941 they provided shelter and care for thousands of refugees who were fleeing Nazi persecution. This included hiding more than 2,000 Jewish men, women, and children from the Germans.

The center of daily life at the monastery was perpetual Adoration of the Blessed Sacrament. Kolbe recognized the evil that was confronting the world and called for constant prayer before the Eucharist.

The rise of evil led Kolbe to place Jesus at the heart of his community. These were his words to the people, "Jesus is the first citizen of Niepokalanow [Kolbe's monastery], the elder Brother and Bridegroom of souls, present in the Eucharist. He makes us brothers. He warms our hearts with mutual love."

Eventually the monastery was shut down. Kolbe was then arrested by the Gestapo and sent to Auschwitz. In July of 1941 a man escaped from the camp. The deputy commander picked ten men to be starved to death in an underground bunker to discourage others from trying to escape. One of the men selected cried out, "My wife! My children!" Kolbe volunteered to take his place.

After two weeks without food or water, Maximilian Kolbe was the only one alive. The guards killed him with a lethal injection so they could reuse the bunker. He died on August 14.

The history of Christianity is paved with sacrifices large and small that echo the love of Jesus' sacrifice on the Cross in every place and time. Self-denial and sacrificing for the sake of others is another rich theme that runs through the lives of the saints.

Our modern times seem addicted to comfort and allergic to sacrifice. Both postures make the Christian life at least difficult and at most impossible. In order to love, and love deeply, we have to be willing to give up some comfort and take on some sacrifice.

Love of comfort is a form of self-worship. Let us set aside our fixation with comfort and worship the one true God by adopting the spirit of sacrifice that Jesus embraced on the Cross.

Our willingness to make sacrifices for those we love is one of the ways we give weight to the words, "I love you." And where does the courage, strength, and grace to make life-giving sacrifices come from? From Jesus in the Eucharist. Saint Maximilian Kolbe wrote, "Jesus, You come to me and unite Yourself intimately to me in the form of nourishment. Your Blood now runs in mine, Your Soul, Incarnate God, compenetrates mine, giving courage and support. What miracles! Who would have ever imagined such!"

Maximilian Kolbe had laid down his life in small ways for other people thousands of times before that day in Auschwitz. You and I may never find ourselves in a situation like that, but each day is filled with opportunities to take someone else's place. Each time we do, that is a Holy Moment. It is a Eucharistic moment. What small sacrifice are you willing to make today for somebody else?

Trust. Surrender. Believe. Receive.

LESSON
There is no love without sacrifice. Love is indispensable for a Christian, and therefore, so is sacrifice. Make small sacrifices each day that clearly demonstrate your love for God and neighbor.

VIRTUE OF THE DAY
Sacrifice: The virtue of sacrifice enhances the meaning of our existence. The ability to set aside our desires and personal preferences, expecting nothing in return, is evidence of the nobility of the human person. Let your selfishness give way to love and you will embrace the sacrifices of daily life enthusiastically.

SPIRITUAL COMMUNION
Jesus,
I believe that You are truly present
in the Most Holy Sacrament of the Eucharist.
Every day I long for more of You.
I love You above all things, and I desire to receive You into my soul.
Since I cannot receive You sacramentally at this moment,
I invite You to come and dwell in my heart.

May this spiritual communion increase my desire for the Eucharist.
You are the healer of my soul.
Take the blindness from my eyes,
the deafness from my ears,
the darkness from my mind,
and the hardness from my heart.
Fill me with the grace, wisdom, and courage to do Your will in all things.
My Lord and my God, draw me close to You, nearer than ever before.
Amen.

THOMAS AQUINAS:
THERE IS A DIFFERENCE
DAY 12

"Set your minds on the things that are above, not on earthly things."
Colossians 3:2

It was a typical Wednesday morning in Naples, Italy. The year was 1273 and it was the Feast of Saint Nicholas. The temperature hovered around fifty degrees, as it mostly does at that time of year, and the burly priest, wearing the same black habit he had worn for years, was doing what he loved more than anything in the world. He was offering Mass.

His focus and commitment were palpable to all those in attendance. The priest was known to have mystical experiences during Mass. Many had seen him burst into tears or become dumbstruck during the consecration. Others had heard stories.

So it wasn't that unusual that on this day, as he consecrated the bread and wine, a vision overcame his senses. Later, some would say he saw Jesus. Others that he was granted a glimpse of the glory of Heaven. The priest himself never explained what happened or described what he saw.

It wasn't the vision that shocked those who knew the priest. It was what he did next. After a lifetime using his unrivaled intellectual genius to write, the priest declared that his work was finished. When his secretary and friend asked him what had happened, he replied, "All that I have written appears to be as so much straw after the things that have been revealed to me."

Now that wouldn't mean much coming from most people, but it was a staggering statement for this particular priest. His name was Thomas Aquinas.

Over the 2,000-year history of Catholicism, Thomas Aquinas is among the greatest theologians and philosophers the Church has known. Many believe his intellectual contribution to be unmatched.

His theological and philosophical works are still studied today in all manner of schools and universities across the world. His *Summa Theologica* is a masterpiece of epic proportions, and yet, after whatever he saw at Mass on that fateful December day, he decided to leave it unfinished. He would die just three months later without penning another word.

Thomas Aquinas had one of the greatest minds in human history. But he was intimately aware of two important truths that allude many great minds.

The first was this: The longest journey we make is from the head to the heart. It is a spiritual journey, a pilgrimage of prayer. We think of the heart as emotional, and it is, but it is also deeply spiritual. This was the second: There is a vast difference between knowing about God and knowing God.

Do you know Jesus or do you just know about Jesus?

Saint Thomas Aquinas wasn't just a brilliant mind. He was a man driven by a deep love for God. He was a man of deep prayer. And at the very center of his life, the source of his wisdom and joy, was the Eucharist.

The same man who used Aristotelian philosophy to define Transubstantiation—the moment the bread and wine become the Body and Blood of Christ—could hardly speak at times during the Mass because he was so moved when he participated in the actual miracle.

Thomas Aquinas' example invites us to ask some powerful questions about our own lives: Am I living my life from the mind? Am I living my life from the heart? Or have I found the delicate balance between the heart and the mind where love and wisdom reside?

One night, in the chapel of the Dominican priory in Naples, a sacristan concealed himself to observe Thomas Aquinas at prayer. He saw Thomas lifted into the air and heard Christ speaking to him from the crucifix on the chapel wall, "Thomas, you have written well of me. What reward will you have?"

"Lord, nothing but yourself," was Thomas' reply.

Anytime we think we want something other than Jesus, we are mistaken, confused, disoriented, disillusioned, or deceived. For it is "in Him that we live, and move, and have our being." (Acts 17:28)

"Love takes up where knowledge leaves off," is what Aquinas observed. As we continue to deepen our relationship with the Eucharist, it is fruitful to expand our knowledge and intellectual understanding of the Eucharist. But let us never forget that it is our relationship with Jesus—True God and True Man—that animates our faith.

As one of the greatest writers of all time, Thomas said it more profoundly than I could ever hope to: "The Eucharist is the Sacrament of Love. It signifies Love. It produces love. The Eucharist is the consummation of the whole spiritual life."

Trust. Surrender. Believe. Receive.

LESSON

Knowing about someone is not the same as knowing a person. Strive to know Jesus more with every passing day.

VIRTUE OF THE DAY

Wisdom: The virtue of wisdom is the good judgment to consider the outcomes and consequences of today's choices on the future—in this life and in eternity. The world is drowning in information and knowledge but starving for wisdom. Wisdom is truth lived.

SPIRITUAL COMMUNION

Jesus,

I believe that You are truly present

in the Most Holy Sacrament of the Eucharist.

Every day I long for more of You.

I love You above all things, and I desire to receive You into my soul.

Since I cannot receive You sacramentally at this moment,

I invite You to come and dwell in my heart.

May this spiritual communion increase my desire for the Eucharist.

You are the healer of my soul.

Take the blindness from my eyes,

the deafness from my ears,

the darkness from my mind,

and the hardness from my heart.

Fill me with the grace, wisdom, and courage to do Your will in all things.

My Lord and my God, draw me close to You, nearer than ever before.

Amen.

SISTER FAUSTINA: DON'T DELAY
DAY 13

"Set your minds on the things that are above, not on earthly things."
Colossians 3:2

Helena Kowalska was a nineteen-year-old Polish girl with a broken heart. She had recently given up her dream of joining the convent. Her family was against it, and she did not have the financial means to enter on her own.

A few months later, on a warm summer night, something mysterious happened. Helena was at a dance with her sister. The party was in full swing when a young man asked her to dance. Determined to move forward with her life, Helena walked out on the dance floor, twirled about, and tried to enjoy the moment.

But suddenly, the music seemed to stop. The dance faded away. And Helena found herself face to face with Jesus. "How long will you keep putting me off?" He said to her. Then, just as quickly as the vision had appeared, it faded away. Helena was understandably shaken and unwilling to continue dancing.

She believed that God had closed the door on her dream of entering the convent. But now, with this direct message from Jesus, her assumption was proven wrong.

Even though every possible obstacle seemed to be in her way, she left home and found a convent willing to open its doors to her. It was there that Helena became known as Sister Maria Faustina.

Before too long, Jesus appeared to Faustina again . . . and again . . . to share just one message: Mercy.

The twentieth century was one of the ugliest and deadliest centuries in human history and, right in the middle of it all, Jesus was sharing a message of mercy through Sister Faustina.

In her journal, Sister Faustina wrote: "All grace flows from mercy, and the last hour abounds with mercy for us. Let no one doubt concerning the goodness of God; even if a person's sins were as dark as night, God's mercy is stronger than our misery. One thing alone is necessary, that the sinner set ajar the door of his heart, be it ever so little, to let in a ray of God's merciful grace, and then God will do the rest."

That message of mercy extended, in a particular way, to the Eucharist.

During one of her visions, Jesus told Sister Faustina, "When I come to a human heart in Holy Communion, my hands are full of all kinds of graces which I want to give to the soul. But souls do not even pay any attention to me; they leave me to myself and busy themselves with other things. Oh, how sad I am that souls do not recognize love! They treat me as a dead object."

A dead object. A piece of bread. A cup of wine. Dead.

When Jesus walked the earth, He made it clear that reception of His Body and Blood was not a symbolic ritual, but that in the Eucharist we indeed receive the real and True Presence of God. He reasserted this truth to Sister Faustina. He is alive, not dead. The bread is not bread, but the very life of God, sent to you out of love and mercy.

In her epic writings about Divine Mercy, Sister Faustina wrote, "You wanted to stay with us, and so you left us yourself in the Sacrament of the Altar, and you opened wide your mercy to us. You opened an inexhaustible spring of mercy for us, giving us your dearest possession, the Blood and Water, that gushed forth from Your Heart."

He wanted to stay with us. Think about that. He wanted to stay with us. He wanted to be here with you. By consecrating yourself to the Eucharist you are becoming an agent of mercy. Beautiful, courageous, loving, transformative, never-ending—mercy.

Trust. Surrender. Believe. Receive.

LESSON

Stop putting God off. Surrender to what He is calling you to do completely and without delay.

VIRTUE OF THE DAY

Mercy: Thomas Aquinas defined the virtue of mercy in his great *Summa Theologiae* as "compassion in our hearts for another person's misery, a compassion which drives us to do what we can to help him." (ST II–II.30.1) Mercy is a form of temporal and spiritual generosity.

SPIRITUAL COMMUNION

Jesus,
I believe that You are truly present
in the Most Holy Sacrament of the Eucharist.
Every day I long for more of You.
I love You above all things, and I desire to receive You into my soul.
Since I cannot receive You sacramentally at this moment,
I invite You to come and dwell in my heart.
May this spiritual communion increase my desire for the Eucharist.
You are the healer of my soul.
Take the blindness from my eyes,
the deafness from my ears,
the darkness from my mind,
and the hardness from my heart.
Fill me with the grace, wisdom, and courage to do Your will in all things.
My Lord and my God, draw me close to You, nearer than ever before.
Amen.

MARY: THE POWER OF YES
DAY 14

"Set your minds on the things that are above, not on earthly things."
Colossians 3:2

One of the fruits of consecration is an expanded awareness of how powerful our "yes" is. Free will is an extraordinary gift. It is the essence of love. The ability to say "yes" carries with it a power and a responsibility that few people in history have reflected upon enough to take seriously. For the most part we take it for granted and misuse this extraordinary ability. But every time you say "yes," it changes you. Forever.

Consecration is about saying "yes" to God. This Consecration to the Eucharist will be a great "yes." One of the greatest "yeses" of your life.

One word. Three letters. "Yes." It all comes down to that in the end. Are we willing to say "yes" to God?

There are some beautiful lines in the Scriptures that sum everything up. On the wall in my children's room is a picture of Noah's ark, and inscribed in the wooden frame are the words "Noah did all that God asked him to do." (Genesis 7:5) That's it. Just do what God asks you to do. At the wedding feast in Cana, Mary said to the servants, "Do whatever He tells you." (John 2:5) Say "yes" to God in everything.

One moment at a time, we are each called to embrace His will. It is monumentally simple, but we find endless ways to complicate and avoid it.

Why don't we passionately seek God's will? Too often I find myself saying "yes" to God begrudgingly. It isn't a generous "yes." I know that, and I know God knows it.

When the angel Gabriel came to Mary to announce that God

wanted her to bear His Son, she gave a complete "yes" in response. In that moment of beautiful surrender, Mary became the first tabernacle to hold the Body and Blood of Jesus the Savior of the World. Each time we receive the Eucharist, we become living tabernacles holding Jesus too.

Mary's "yes" echoes throughout history. This was the great "yes." Her humble words of surrender, "Be it done unto me according to your word," (Luke 1:38) is a spirituality unto itself. Seeking and doing the will of God has been the path of saints for over 2,000 years.

While there is an endless amount of inspiration to be gleaned from Mary's surrender, it is what happened next that opens our eyes to what it really means to carry Jesus into the world.

Mary had just been told that she was to become the mother of God, to carry the Messiah in her womb, and yet her first thought was for others. How often is your first thought for others? We read in the Scriptures that Mary "arose and went with all haste" to her cousin Elizabeth (Luke 1:39), who Mary had just discovered was pregnant in her old age with John the Baptist.

When was the last time you responded to your spouse, parents, or customers "with all haste"? When your husband or wife asks you to do something, or when your manager at work asks you to do a little extra, do you respond with an enthusiasm to serve? We live in an age of meaninglessness because we have lost sight of the fact that our very purpose is to serve God and others. And the more we think about ourselves the unhappier we become.

Mary rushed off to serve Elizabeth. It was her first reaction. Her instinctive response. Too often my first reaction is one of selfishness: "I don't feel like it." "I'll do it later." "Can't someone else take care of it?" But Mary had an instinct to serve, an ingrained humility.

God wants to fill us with a holy sense of urgency. Every day people are losing hope. God seems far from them. They feel forgotten, invisible, unloved. So much is at stake. Mary wants to teach us to love God and neighbor with this holy sense of urgency.

And still, there is another lesson here for us. The Scriptures tell us that when Mary greeted Elizabeth, the child John the Baptist leapt for joy in her womb. Even in the womb, John the Baptist recognized he was in the presence of God.

There is a connection between this passage and an Old Testament passage in which David dances for joy before the Ark of the Covenant. For the Jewish people the Ark of the Covenant was God's dwelling place among them. Just as David danced for joy in the presence of God, we now see John the Baptist dancing for joy in the presence of God. At that moment, Mary was a human tabernacle—the new Ark of the Covenant. The infant John the Baptist already had the extraordinary spiritual awareness to recognize that astounding truth and danced for joy.

Do you bring joy to people's lives? Do people experience joy when they hear you are coming to visit? When you mindfully carry Jesus with you everywhere you go, you will become an ambassador of joy.

The Ark of the Covenant was God's dwelling place on earth. Mary's body was now God's dwelling place on earth. And when you receive Jesus in the Eucharist you become God's dwelling place on earth.

The problem is we have lost our senses. This is a common saying, but what does it mean? It means: unable to find one's way or ascertain one's whereabouts; confused, bewildered, or helpless. We have truly lost our spiritual senses. We are no longer able to recognize the presence of God. Our spiritual senses have been dulled and drowned out by the chaos of our lives. Let's beg God to awaken and sharpen our spiritual senses so we can recognize

Him in every moment and dance for joy.

With every little "yes" we give God, our spiritual senses will be awakened, restored, sharpened, strengthened. Say "yes" to God today in as many little ways possible. This way you will be ready when a big "yes" is required of you. How will you do it? By realizing where the strength comes from. Can you do it by yourself? No. But you can do it. Remind yourself: "I can do all things through Christ who strengthens me." (Philippians 4:13)

Trust. Surrender. Believe. Receive.

LESSON
Say "yes" to God in all things. Actively seek out opportunities to say "yes" to God throughout the day.

VIRTUE OF THE DAY
Humility: The virtue of humility is the starting point of the spiritual life. Small deeds done with humility are infinitely more pleasing to God than great deeds done out of pride. Self-knowledge will lead humility to take root in your life and soul. The inner dignity born of humility is astoundingly attractive.

SPIRITUAL COMMUNION
Jesus,
I believe that You are truly present
in the Most Holy Sacrament of the Eucharist.
Every day I long for more of You.
I love You above all things, and I desire to receive You into my soul.
Since I cannot receive You sacramentally at this moment,
I invite You to come and dwell in my heart.
May this spiritual communion increase my desire for the Eucharist.
You are the healer of my soul.
Take the blindness from my eyes,

the deafness from my ears,
the darkness from my mind,
and the hardness from my heart.
Fill me with the grace, wisdom, and courage to do Your will in all
things.
My Lord and my God, draw me close to You, nearer than ever before.
Amen.

WEEK THREE

The Eucharist
and
You

ALL YOU WHO NEED REST
DAY 15

"I can do all things through Christ who strengthens me."
Philippians 4:13

There is a lot of talk these days about boundaries. It's a psychological term that refers to setting realistic limits for participation in a relationship or activity. These limits are necessary to protect the integrity of an individual or relationship.

Relationships need boundaries to remain healthy. Our lives also need boundaries to remain healthy. Do you set realistic limits for your participation in life?

God in His ever-loving providence gave us the Sabbath as the first boundary, but also as the boundary that gives us the clarity to set all other boundaries.

Saint Irenaeus observed, "The glory of God is man fully alive." What would your life look like if you were "fully alive?" What would have to be true for you to become fully alive?

God is calling you to wholeness and holiness. Consider the four aspects of the human person: physical, emotional, intellectual, and spiritual. In which of these areas are you thriving? In which are you just surviving?

And what prevents you from thriving? I suspect it is the sheer busyness of your life, the noise and complexity of modern life, the stress induced by never-ending urgency.

Compare that to Jesus' invitation, "Come to me, all you who are weary and burdened, and I will give you rest. Take my yoke upon you and learn from me, for I am gentle and humble of heart, and you will find rest for your souls. For my yoke is easy and my burden is light." (Matthew 11:28–30) This is one of the most beautiful and compassionate moments in the Scriptures.

Most of us are weary and burdened. Most of us don't find that burden to be light. And most of us are not getting the rest we need to thrive in every area of life.

Rest is a divine activity. God rested on the seventh day (Genesis 2:2), not because He was tired, but because He knew we would get tired and need rest. God rested on the seventh day to set a boundary between the demands of the world and our very human needs. God rested on the seventh day because He was teaching us an essential element necessary to thrive.

Modern scientific research shows that people are most satisfied in life when they find a rhythm of working intensely for a period, and then completely unplugging and resting for a period. Rest reduces stress by activating the parasympathetic nervous system, the opposite of the sympathetic nervous system which is responsible for the fight or flight response. Do you ever feel like the whole world is in fight or flight mode? This is why. We are neglecting our legitimate need for meaningful rest. Brain data also shows that periods of rest boost creativity. How often has the solution to a problem come to you when you go for a walk or step away from your work for an extended period? Rest improves productivity and enhances your ability to make sound decisions. Have you ever noticed that people make poor decisions when they are exhausted? And the endless benefits of great sleep are well documented and ignored by most people.

You have an essential need for rest. It is undeniable. Are you ignoring it? It is time to set appropriate boundaries for your life by establishing an authentic Sabbath experience.

We inherited the Sabbath tradition from our Jewish spiritual ancestors. The Jewish Sabbath is observed from sundown on Friday to sundown on Saturday. Catholics observe the Sabbath on Sunday. But I know many Catholics, especially those with demanding professional responsibilities, who practice the Sabbath from sundown on Saturday to sundown on Sunday. This allows them to take a couple of hours Sunday night to prepare for the week ahead.

Honoring the Sabbath sets up the necessary boundaries to fully experience receiving Jesus in the Eucharist during Sunday Mass. When we live within those boundaries and follow God's model of rest, the spiritual fruits we experience are extraordinary.

God is interested in the whole person, not just the spiritual aspect, and so, the Sabbath also creates the opportunity for your rest and restoration as a whole person. You may find it helpful to approach the Sabbath with the four aspects of the human person in mind: physical, emotional, intellectual, and spiritual.

Carefree timelessness is essential for a relationship to thrive. No relationship can thrive without restful time together without an agenda. The Sabbath is an opportunity for carefree timelessness with God and each other.

Most people are bored and tired at Mass because they are bored and tired with their lives. When we honor the Sabbath everything changes. From this place of rest and renewal we will approach the Eucharist with childlike awe and enthusiasm. Only then will we be able to comprehend what the saints have shared with us about the Eucharist, like this reflection from Padre Pio: "Every Holy Mass, heard with devotion, produces in our soul marvelous effects, abundant spiritual and material graces which we cannot fathom. It is easier for the earth to exist without the sun than without the Holy Sacrifice of the Mass!"

The Eucharist is the ultimate form of restoration, and it is best experienced in the context of the Sabbath rest. It is time we accepted this gift that God has been trying to give to humanity since the beginning of time.

Trust. Surrender. Believe. Receive.

LESSON

Set appropriate boundaries for your life by establishing an authentic Sabbath experience.

VIRTUE OF THE DAY

Rest: The virtue of rest involves taking a break from the activities of life that wear us out and grind us down, to give God a chance to fill us up and build us up. Through rest, you make space in your life for more meaningful activities by taking a break from the less meaningful mundane activity of your life.

SPIRITUAL COMMUNION

Jesus,
I believe that You are truly present
in the Most Holy Sacrament of the Eucharist.
Every day I long for more of You.
I love You above all things, and I desire to receive You into my soul.
Since I cannot receive You sacramentally at this moment,
I invite You to come and dwell in my heart.
May this spiritual communion increase my desire for the Eucharist.
You are the healer of my soul.
Take the blindness from my eyes,
the deafness from my ears,
the darkness from my mind,
and the hardness from my heart.
Fill me with the grace, wisdom, and courage to do Your will in all things.
My Lord and my God, draw me close to You, nearer than ever before.
Amen.

HEALER OF MY SOUL
DAY 16

"I can do all things through Christ who strengthens me."
Philippians 4:13

Who do you know who needs what this woman needed?

"There was a woman who had been suffering from hemorrhages for twelve years and though she had spent all she had on physicians no one could cure her. She came up behind Jesus and touched the fringe of his clothes, and immediately her hemorrhage stopped. Then Jesus asked, 'Who touched me?' When all denied it, Peter said, 'Master the crowds surround you and press in on you.' But Jesus said, 'Someone touched me for I noticed that power had gone out from me.' When the woman saw that she could not remain hidden she came trembling and falling down before him she declared in the presence of all the people why she had touched him and how she had been immediately healed. He said to her 'Daughter your faith has made you well go in peace.'" (Luke 8:43–48)

Jesus is always healing people. Think about the Gospels. One thing we witness Him doing over and over again is healing men, women, and children. He made the blind see, gave hearing to the deaf, cured the paralyzed, fed the hungry, comforted the afflicted, counseled the worried and anxious, liberated the possessed, cleansed lepers, forgave those burdened with guilt and shame, gave speech to those who could not speak, and even raised Lazarus from the dead.

The mistake we make is we set these stories and the people in them apart from ourselves. We don't think we need healing. If we are not blind, when we hear the story of Jesus giving sight to the blind man Bartimaeus, we don't think of ourselves. If we are not paralyzed, when we hear the story of Jesus healing the paralytic, we don't think of ourselves. If we are not deaf, when we hear the story of Jesus restoring the hearing of the deaf, we don't think of ourselves. And it would never occur to us to see ourselves in the possessed man, woman, or child.

But we are blind. We are paralyzed. We are deaf. We are possessed. It may manifest in different ways and to different degrees, but we are. We are all blind and deaf and paralyzed and hungry. We all need to be comforted in our afflictions. We need to be counseled in our worries and anxiety. We all need to be liberated from spirits that possess us. We are all lepers in need of cleansing. We all need to be forgiven for the mistakes and sins and regrets that burden us with guilt and shame. We all need to be given a voice in situations where we find it hard to speak up. And in some way or another, some part of us, or some aspect of our lives needs to be raised from the dead.

We all need healing. Desperately.

When I asked you earlier: "Who do you know who needs what this woman needed?" who came to mind? You probably didn't think of yourself, but your need for healing is great.

Now, think about the story from Luke's Gospel above again, but this time think about it in the context of the Eucharist. This poor woman had been bleeding for twelve years, she'd heard about Jesus, and she had been waiting for Him to come to her town, or perhaps she went out searching for Him. Her faith was such that she didn't need a lot of attention. Her ego was in check. Filled with faith and humility, she believed that if she could just touch Jesus' cloak she would be healed.

Here's my question: What would she have believed possible if she had been able to receive Jesus in the Eucharist—Body, Blood, Soul, and Divinity? What would she have believed possible if she had been able to experience the Eucharistic Glory of consuming the glorified Christ, who rose from the dead, under the appearances of bread and wine?

How do you think she would respond if she could experience the Eucharistic Glory that most Catholics take for granted on Sunday? And not just her, but pick any of the dozens of people throughout the Gospel who approach Jesus humbly seeking His help: How would they respond to the possibility and opportunity of the Eucharist?

Did you notice what I said earlier? Jesus *is* always healing people. I didn't say Jesus *was* always healing people because that would have been a half-truth.

I don't know what form your need for healing takes, but I do know who can do the healing: Jesus—the carpenter from Nazareth, the itinerant preacher, the Son of God, the King of Kings and the Lord of Lords, the Lamb of God, the new Adam, the Messiah, the Alpha and the Omega, the Chosen One, the Light of the World, the God-Man who wants good things for us more than we want them for ourselves, the healer of our souls.

What would happen if you went to Church next Sunday looking for healing in the same way that this woman sought Jesus out to be healed? What would happen if you brought that broken and difficult part of your life to Jesus in the Eucharist? Do you believe that Jesus can heal you? Don't worry about whether He will or not for now. Just focus on believing that He can.

"Jesus has the power not only to heal, but also to forgive sins. He has come to heal the whole person, soul and body. He is the physician the sick need. His compassion toward all who suffer goes so far that He identifies Himself with them: 'I was sick and you visited me.'" (CCCC 1503) Jesus is your personal healer.

Before we began day one of this journey, in the introduction, I spoke about a Muslim man I met many years ago. I asked him if he believed he could consume his God under the guise of bread, what would he do to receive that bread. Do you remember what he said to me?

"I would crawl naked over red-hot broken glass." That's what he said. Red-hot broken glass. It is time we all rediscover the healing power of the Eucharist.

Trust. Surrender. Believe. Receive.

LESSON

We are blind. We are paralyzed. We are deaf. We are possessed. Ask Jesus in the Eucharist to heal you.

VIRTUE OF THE DAY

Trust: The virtue of trust is in many ways an acknowledgment of the reality that God is in control. It is also a belief that God has a plan for our lives and will provide for us in that plan. One of the most practical ways to grow in the virtue of trust is to become more trustworthy. Trust determines how we participate in relationships. Who we trust reveals our character. The gift of trust is a tranquil soul.

SPIRITUAL COMMUNION

Jesus,
I believe that You are truly present
in the Most Holy Sacrament of the Eucharist.
Every day I long for more of You.
I love You above all things, and I desire to receive You into my soul.
Since I cannot receive You sacramentally at this moment,
I invite You to come and dwell in my heart.
May this spiritual communion increase my desire for the Eucharist.
You are the healer of my soul.
Take the blindness from my eyes,
the deafness from my ears,

the darkness from my mind,
and the hardness from my heart.
Fill me with the grace, wisdom, and courage to do Your will in all
things.
My Lord and my God, draw me close to You, nearer than ever before.
Amen.

IS SACRIFICE THE ANSWER?
DAY 17

"I can do all things through Christ who strengthens me."
Philippians 4:13

If someone knew the best way to do something and that something was an important part of your life, wouldn't you want to learn everything you could from that person? Most reasonable and rational people would say yes. So, what would you say if I told you, at this time when the divorce rate among Catholics is generally considered to be around 50 percent, there was a city on this planet with no divorces. Not less, not half, not very few—none. You would think everyone would want to know their secret.

Siroki-Brijeg is the city with no divorce. Located in Bosnia-Herzegovina, there are 30,000 inhabitants and not a single recorded case of divorce in living memory.

For centuries these people were persecuted for their Catholic faith. They suffered the invasions of Muslim Turks, they suffered Nazi occupation and genocide, and more recently they have suffered at the hands of Communist atheists. Famine, war, cultural strife, and unending political upheaval stain almost every page of their history books.

They have suffered. And through that suffering they have learned an epic lesson: sacrifice and salvation are inseparably connected.

What does all this have to do with marriage and divorce? Out of these intense and prolonged experiences of suffering, they developed a unique wedding ritual.

On the day of their wedding, the bride and groom bring a crucifix to the church. The priest blesses it and tells the couple: "You have found your cross. And it is a cross to be loved, to be carried, a cross not to be thrown away, but to be cherished."

When it comes time for the exchange of vows, the bride places her right hand on the crucifix and the groom places his hand over hers. The priest wraps his stole around their hands and around the cross.

After saying their vows, the bride and groom do not kiss one another. They both kiss Jesus on the Cross—only then do they kiss each other.

When the ceremony is over, the now-married couple brings the crucifix to their home and displays it prominently. From that day on, they bring their hopes, dreams, struggles, worries, gratitude, and sorrows and lay them at the foot of the Cross. When they have children, they present their children to Jesus on the Cross. It becomes the centerpiece of their spiritual life as a couple, and as a family. Every night before going to bed, the children kiss Jesus goodnight, just as their parents kissed Him on the day they united their souls as one in marriage.

Love and sacrifice are inseparable. Suffering and salvation are inseparable. In a fallen world, broken by selfishness and bent out of shape by pride, greed, wrath, envy, lust, sloth and gluttony, love requires sacrifice.

In relationships among fallen people constantly tempted to selfishness and pride, love and sacrifice go hand in hand. Married couples need to know this better than most, but every truly loving relationship in our lives is stitched together by an endless stream of sacrifices. The moment you stop sacrificing for the other person in a relationship is the moment that relationship begins to die.

When Jesus gave up His life on the Cross to save us, it was the ultimate act of love. This alone teaches us something about love at the foundational level. The ultimate act of love was an act of total sacrifice. He held nothing back.

We live in a time when there is very rarely alignment between what a person says and what a person does. But Jesus' life was in complete conformity with His teachings. There was a total alignment between who He was, what He taught, and how He chose to live His life.

This is what He said, "Greater love has no man than this, that a man lay down his life for his friends." (John 15:13) And this is what He did, "They took Jesus and led Him away. And carrying His own Cross, went out to a place called Golgotha, where they crucified Him." (John 19:17-18) What He said and what He did were perfectly integrated. This is what it means to live with integrity, to align what we do with what we say and what we believe.

Every Mass is an opportunity to learn from Jesus' sacrifice on the Cross.

Each time we receive the Eucharist, we receive the Body and Blood of Jesus. Not a symbol of it. It is the same body He sacrificed on the Cross, the same blood He poured out with indescribable love. This is the essence of the Eucharist, it is Jesus offering Himself up for you on the Cross, an absolute demonstration of His love for you now and for all eternity.

The Cross is Jesus' ultimate teaching. It is the ultimate masterclass. The wisdom we can glean from Jesus' Crucifixion has broad applications to every aspect of our lives. But what is clear is that the people of Siroki-Brijeg have adopted the crucifixion as a masterclass on marriage.

When we receive the Eucharist, which is born from the masterclass of the Cross, we are given the grace, courage, wisdom, and fortitude to offer up our own sufferings for those we love and all in need.

There is no path to happiness in this life unless you can make sense of suffering, and Christianity is the only religion or philosophy that understands the transformative value of suffering. While the whole world is doing everything it can to avoid and drown out their pain and suffering, we are reminded each Sunday at Mass that our pain and suffering have tremendous value when united to the pain and suffering of Jesus on the Cross.

Separated from Jesus, our pain and suffering become meaningless, and that is why life is so depressing for so many in a world that has rejected God and the idea that suffering has value.

Willing sacrifice out of love is a path most people have never tried. It is a path most married couples have never been taught. And it is a path that is essential if we are going to find our way back to thriving in this world.

Sacrificial love brings meaning to our lives in a culture of meaninglessness. It binds us together in a world intent on tearing everyone apart. It provides healing in a culture overwhelmed with wounds.

Choose a relationship in your life that is struggling and pour into it the unmitigated love of daily sacrifice.

Every Sunday at Mass we see before us the secret to lasting relationships represented on the altar. There is a direct connection between the most momentous event in human history and your marriage, friendships, and every meaningful relationship in your life. It is the loving sacrifice.

Jesus modeled self-sacrifice, so that we could learn from Him. The Mass models that self-sacrifice for us to continue to learn from, and to provide an opportunity to go deeper into the counterintuitive genius of God's ways. Saint Jerome famously observed, "Ignorance of the Bible is ignorance of Jesus." I would add, in a world where people seem obsessed with finding the easiest path, "Ignorance of the Cross is ignorance of Jesus."

We have turned away from referring to our Eucharistic gathering as the Sacrifice of the Mass in favor of calling it the Celebration of the Mass. Words matter. They direct our thoughts, and our thoughts direct our actions. The Mass is both a sacrifice and a celebration, but when we forget that it is only because of the sacrifice that we have something to celebrate, we raise up generations of people who crave celebration and are ill prepared to face the inevitable sacrifices of life.

There is no love without sacrifice. Inject sacrifice into any relationship where love has evaporated and allow the fruits of Jesus' sacrifice on the Cross to breathe new life into that relationship.

For so long we have all been looking for answers. Maybe sacrifice is the answer we have all been looking for but have refused to adopt.

Trust. Surrender. Believe. Receive.

LESSON

There is no love without sacrifice. The Cross is Jesus' ultimate teaching. It is the ultimate masterclass on love. Inject sacrifice into any relationship and allow the fruits of Jesus' sacrifice on the Cross to breathe new life into that relationship.

VIRTUE OF THE DAY

Kindness: The virtue of kindness is the excellence of character that imbues every thought, word, and action with goodness. It reveals the essence of our humanity in our ability to bring the goodness of God into any situation. Never underestimate the value of a kind word, thought, or deed. The power of simple kindness is unfathomable. The future of humanity is dependent on the selfless caring we call kindness.

SPIRITUAL COMMUNION

Jesus,
I believe that You are truly present
in the Most Holy Sacrament of the Eucharist.
Every day I long for more of You.
I love You above all things, and I desire to receive You into my soul.
Since I cannot receive You sacramentally at this moment,
I invite You to come and dwell in my heart.
May this spiritual communion increase my desire for the Eucharist.
You are the healer of my soul.
Take the blindness from my eyes,
the deafness from my ears,
the darkness from my mind,
and the hardness from my heart.
Fill me with the grace, wisdom, and courage to do Your will in all things.
My Lord and my God, draw me close to You, nearer than ever before.
Amen.

THE FRUITS OF THE EUCHARIST
DAY 18

"I can do all things through Christ who strengthens me."
Philippians 4:13

"What do I get out of it?" he said. I was a little stunned at first, but then I realized, he wasn't being rude. The tone of his voice was quite sincere. It was just raw human nature. And now I could see why he had been resisting. He simply couldn't see how my proposal was going to benefit him. It was. I just needed to show him that. And then later I realized, we are all like that sometimes.

Sometimes we need to know how something will benefit us. And that's okay. So, let's talk about some more of the benefits of the Eucharist.

When was the last time you did something that you knew wasn't good for you? Why did you do it? Think of reasons, come up with excuses, but at the end of the day it comes down to this: You have disordered desires that are difficult to control. The grace of the Eucharist can help with that.

There's an agonizing and relatable moment in Saint Paul's letter to the Romans where he says, "I do not understand my own actions. For I do not do the good I want, but the evil I do not want is what I do... I can will what is right, but I cannot do it." (Romans 7:15, 19)

Have you ever felt that struggle? You are standing at the moment of decision. You know what is good and right. You know it will ultimately make you happier. You know it's better for you. And yet, you find yourself doing what is bad anyway. This can be incredibly frustrating, and the grace of the Eucharist can help with this too.

You aren't alone. This happens to everyone more often than

we care to admit. We know we should pray instead of watching another episode of TV. . . but there we are on the couch again. We know it would be better to eat the salad instead of the cheeseburger. . . but before we know it, we're ordering a double with fries. We feel the tug to listen to our children or spouse. . . but almost without thinking our phone is out and we are checking messages.

Jesus diagnoses the problem for us when He says, "The spirit is willing, but the flesh is weak." (Matthew 26:41) We cannot escape our bodies and willpower alone isn't enough to overcome every temptation, so we are stuck in this dilemma.

The good news is that Jesus provided a way to conquer these situations. Not with our strength, but with His. He offered His own flesh to energize our souls and give us the grace we need to turn from what is bad for us and do what is good. Each time you receive the Eucharist, Jesus gives you extraordinary gifts to help you live the life you were made for. Here is a short list of some of the fruits and gifts that flow into your soul each time you receive the Eucharist:

Friendship with Jesus.

Desire to know and do the will of God.

Cleansing of venial sin.

Hunger for virtue.

Grace to avoid sin in the future.

A heart that listens to the Holy Spirit.

Desire to know and love God.

Take a few minutes to reflect on this list. It is an incredible list of gifts. Which of these don't you need? Think about situations in your life that went wrong, which of these gifts could have helped you prevent those outcomes? Which do you need right now in your life? Are you in a situation right now that would benefit from one of these gifts? Ask Jesus to flood your soul with that particular gift next time you receive the Eucharist.

We should yearn for these more than any of the things we yearn for. Saint John Bosco observed, "Do you want many graces? Go and visit the Blessed Sacrament often. Do you want few graces? Visit the Blessed Sacrament rarely. Do you want none at all? Then never pay a visit to the Blessed Sacrament."

The beautiful thing about these gifts is how relevant they are to our day to day lives. The Catholic Church and the Mass are often accused of being irrelevant, but it's a lie. This list of gifts and fruits that flow from the Eucharist to you is incredibly practical. Embrace them and you will have better relationships, do your best work ever, and have more clarity around every decision you make for the rest of your life.

These fruits of the Eucharist will help you become a-better-version-of-yourself each day. They will help you become all God created you to be. The grace of the Eucharist will help you do the next right thing. Do the next right thing often enough for long enough and amazing things will begin to happen.

Trust. Surrender. Believe. Receive.

LESSON
We all experience a struggle between what we want to do and what we are called to do. We all have disordered desires that need to be controlled. The grace and gifts of the Eucharist allow us to navigate these struggles. Which fruit of the Eucharist do you need right now in your life? Next time you receive the Eucharist, ask Jesus to flood your soul with that particular gift.

VIRTUE OF THE DAY
Receptivity: The virtue of receptivity involves opening our hearts, minds, bodies, and souls completely to God and allowing Him to work unimpeded on our souls and in our lives.

SPIRITUAL COMMUNION

Jesus,

I believe that You are truly present
in the Most Holy Sacrament of the Eucharist.
Every day I long for more of You.
I love You above all things, and I desire to receive You into my soul.
Since I cannot receive You sacramentally at this moment,
I invite You to come and dwell in my heart.
May this spiritual communion increase my desire for the Eucharist.
You are the healer of my soul.
Take the blindness from my eyes,
the deafness from my ears,
the darkness from my mind,
and the hardness from my heart.
Fill me with the grace, wisdom, and courage to do Your will in all
things.
My Lord and my God, draw me close to You, nearer than ever before.
Amen.

FIRST, LAST AND ONLY
DAY 19

"I can do all things through Christ who strengthens me."
Philippians 4:13

My boys love baseball and their passion for the game is contagious, so I have become fascinated with the game and all the life lessons it teaches. We recently saw a great player in his last game and I wondered what it was like for him to know he was walking out onto that field for the last time. He had been doing it since he was a child. He loved it. But now it was coming to an end. And what would he give to play one more game, one more series, one more season? But he can't. Sooner or later, all baseball players are told they can't play anymore. Some are told when they are children, others in high school, some in college or the minor leagues, and some after a rich and full professional career. The day can be pushed off with talent and effort, but eventually it will still come.

Think about your favorite sport and your favorite player in the history of that sport. What do you think it was like for them to play their last game? What sort of emotion do you think filled them? And what sort of longing do they still carry for the game? These are powerful experiences and emotions, and still, it is just a game. There are things that are much more important.

Ávila is a small city in the rolling hill country one hour northwest of Madrid in Spain. This is the birthplace of Saint Teresa of Ávila, one of the greatest Catholic mystics and writers of all time. She wrote extensively on many topics and often reflected on her love and appreciation for the Eucharist:

"Jesus realizes that we are weak and knows that the laborers must be nourished with such food."

"Do you think this heavenly food fails to provide sustenance, even for these bodies, that it is not a great medicine even for bodily ills? I know that it is. The wonders this most sacred bread effects in those who worthily receive it are well known."

There is a church in Ávila, built on the site of Teresa's childhood home. In the sacristy where the priests prepare for Mass there is a large wooden crucifix on the wall. The crucifix is surrounded by these words, which have been painted on the wall.

"Priest of Jesus Christ, celebrate this Holy Mass as if it were your first Mass, your last Mass, your only Mass."

Now, let me ask you a question: If you could only go to Mass once in your entire life, if you could only receive the Eucharist once, how satisfied or dissatisfied would you be with how you participated in Mass last Sunday?

So, this is my challenge to you today. From now on, each time you go to Mass, participate as if it were your first Mass, your last Mass, your only Mass.

Imagine you could only participate in Mass one more time before meeting God for the Final Judgment. How would you prepare? What would you wear? What intentions would you bring to that Mass? Who would you pray for knowing you wouldn't see them again in this lifetime?

I don't know when your last Mass will be. But I do know the best way to prepare yourself for that day is to approach each Mass you are blessed to attend as if it were your first, last, and only.

Trust. Surrender. Believe. Receive.

LESSON

Every time you go to Mass, participate as if it were your first Communion, your last Communion, your only Communion.

VIRTUE OF THE DAY

Preparedness: The virtue of preparedness is a state of readiness, especially for death, judgment, and Heaven.

SPIRITUAL COMMUNION

Jesus,

I believe that You are truly present

in the Most Holy Sacrament of the Eucharist.

Every day I long for more of You.

I love You above all things, and I desire to receive You into my soul.

Since I cannot receive You sacramentally at this moment,

I invite You to come and dwell in my heart.

May this spiritual communion increase my desire for the Eucharist.

You are the healer of my soul.

Take the blindness from my eyes,

the deafness from my ears,

the darkness from my mind,

and the hardness from my heart.

Fill me with the grace, wisdom, and courage to do Your will in all things.

My Lord and my God, draw me close to You, nearer than ever before.

Amen.

LOVE REARRANGES OUR PRIORITIES
DAY 20

"I can do all things through Christ who strengthens me."
Philippians 4:13

Have you ever noticed that when people fall in love their priorities change? If a close friend falls in love, you will probably discover she has less time to spend with you because her priority is to spend time with her love interest. It isn't personal. It's natural and normal. Why? Love rearranges our priorities. And our priorities reveal who and what we love.

When I go to Mass, something I have noticed over and again is that when I listen deeply to the Gospel, and reflect on how to apply it to my life, it always challenges me to rearrange my priorities. The Gospel is an invitation to love, and if we accept that invitation our priorities will inevitably change.

This consecration is also an invitation to love the Eucharist more deeply, more completely, than ever before. And the result of this journey will be shifting priorities.

Many people lose friends as they grow spiritually. I don't say that to upset you, but rather to make you aware of a situation you may encounter, so you can make sense of it when it arrives. Our priorities change as we grow spiritually, and so we become less interested in doing things that don't help us to keep growing. This may include things we loved doing in the past. And if it was something we enjoyed doing with friends, it might be hard for them to understand why our interests have changed. This is an opportunity to share with them the beautiful new path you have discovered. Some people will be hungry to learn more about what you have experienced, and others will be resistant. Some people may even reject you because your mere presence challenges them to change and grow.

You will experience the same pull of the Holy Spirit in the other direction. When I am around a holy person, someone who is humble and really striving to grow spiritually, I feel that pull. That person's presence challenges me to refine my priorities even more. Sometimes I am hungry for that, and sometimes I am resistant. But the Holy Spirit is stirring within me, trying to get my attention, to lead and guide me to new heights.

How are your priorities shifting as you journey through this thirty-three-day consecration? What's more important to you than it was twenty days ago? What's less important?

The Eucharistic Presence of God rearranges our priorities. As a disciple of Jesus, one aspect of the Eucharistic Glory we are invited to experience is sitting at His feet and allowing Him to guide and direct our lives.

Stop by church today for a few minutes if you can. Sit with God and allow Him to rearrange your priorities. You will never be happier than when you let God set the priorities and agenda for your life.

Trust. Surrender. Believe. Receive.

LESSON
Love rearranges our priorities. Our priorities reveal who and what we love.

VIRTUE OF THE DAY
Love: The virtue of love allows us to care for another even more than we care for our own self. It is an overflow of the goodness that God places in your heart. Love gives us the grace to make large and small sacrifices without harboring any ill will or resentment toward the object of our love. With every act of love, with every sacrifice for love's sake, our capacity to love grows.

SPIRITUAL COMMUNION

Jesus,
I believe that You are truly present
in the Most Holy Sacrament of the Eucharist.
Every day I long for more of You.
I love You above all things, and I desire to receive You into my soul.
Since I cannot receive You sacramentally at this moment,
I invite You to come and dwell in my heart.
May this spiritual communion increase my desire for the Eucharist.
You are the healer of my soul.
Take the blindness from my eyes,
the deafness from my ears,
the darkness from my mind,
and the hardness from my heart.
Fill me with the grace, wisdom, and courage to do Your will in all things.
My Lord and my God, draw me close to You, nearer than ever before.
Amen.

OUR DAILY BREAD
DAY 21

"I can do all things through Christ who strengthens me."
Philippians 4:13

An organization without a strategic plan is likely to massively underperform or fail. The same is true of an individual's spiritual life. Where there is no plan, progress will be hampered. Toward the end of each year, I encourage leaders to gather their teams and discuss this question: What is the one thing that would change everything? This consecration is your one thing now, but I would like to encourage you to be constantly thinking about this question in relation to your spiritual life: What is the one thing that would change everything?

Consecration to the Eucharist created a huge paradigm shift in my spiritual life. And there have been other singular habits that had outsized impact over the years. The first was when I started stopping by church to pray for ten minutes a day each morning when I was in high school. My spiritual mentor had challenged me to do this. The second was the first time I really read the Gospels for fifteen minutes each day. The third was daily Mass.

I didn't go every day. When I was about sixteen, my spiritual mentor had challenged me to go to daily Mass one day each week, so I began attending Mass on Tuesday evenings at our parish. It was at Mass during the week that I discovered the genius of Catholicism and the beauty of the Mass. It was at these quiet and intimate daily Mass experiences that this sacred ritual really began to ignite my love for Catholicism. I would follow the opening prayer, the readings, and the closing prayer in my missal, and the words began to probe my heart and ignite the fire in my soul. By some grace, I started to listen to the prayers of the Mass, really listen, and it was like the pieces of a puzzle coming together. It was only then that I began to see the incredible vision God has for our lives, for His Church, and for the world.

Over the past three decades, many of the most powerful experiences of Mass I have been blessed with have been in small groups: on a fishing boat on the Sea of Galilee, in the Portiuncula in Assisi, in the Catacombs beneath the streets of Rome, in a side chapel at Maynooth College, in the crypt of Sacre Coeur, and in the tiny chapel in the Solar da Marta hotel in Fatima.

Now I would like to ask you something. Would your life be better if you went to Mass every day? I understand that it may not be possible, but don't completely dismiss it. The devil discourages us by leading us toward all-or-nothing thinking. This is not an attempt to coerce you into doing something. I don't want it to make you feel bad about yourself. Nor do I want to put undue pressure on your life. But don't let what you can't do blind you to what you can do. We need to learn to be honest about the best path, even if we cannot walk that path at this time in our lives. This honesty liberates us to genuinely explore the question: What is possible?

When you ask this question, you may discover that you can go to daily Mass one day each week. Great. Do it. Try to go on the same day each week and make it a holy ritual. "The Lord delights in every little step you take," was Saint Francis de Sales' observation. Take your next step, however small. Take it.

As you consider what is possible in the context of daily Mass, I want to lay before you three challenges today. The first is the same my spiritual mentor presented to me: start going to daily Mass one day each week. The second is to choose one week each year and go to Mass every day for a week. The third is to make the Spiritual Communion we have been praying each day at the end of these reflections a part of your daily routine of prayer every day after we finish this thirty-three-day journey to your

Eucharistic Consecration.

This will forever change the way you experience the Our Father when you pray, "Give us this day, our daily bread."

What is the one thing that would change everything? This is the question we began today with. The answer is a daily encounter with the Eucharist. Whether that is attending Mass, stopping by a church to pray before the tabernacle, or praying a Spiritual Communion, decide here and now, today, once and for all, that every day for the rest of your life you will have a daily encounter with the Eucharist.

Trust. Surrender. Believe. Receive.

LESSON

Decide today to have a daily encounter with the Eucharist every day for the rest of your life.

VIRTUE OF THE DAY

Devotion: The virtue of devotion consists of loyal, loving, consistent, and enthusiastic desire to please God in all things. It is a specifically religious act, chosen deliberately and freely, and directed toward God. Who or what would an outside observer deduce you are devoted to? Too many people misplace their devotion. Be careful not to misplace yours. To give something that belongs to God to anyone or anything else is a grave disorder.

SPIRITUAL COMMUNION

Jesus,
I believe that You are truly present
in the Most Holy Sacrament of the Eucharist.
Every day I long for more of You.
I love You above all things, and I desire to receive You into my soul.
Since I cannot receive You sacramentally at this moment,

I invite You to come and dwell in my heart.

May this spiritual communion increase my desire for the Eucharist.

You are the healer of my soul.

Take the blindness from my eyes,

the deafness from my ears,

the darkness from my mind,

and the hardness from my heart.

Fill me with the grace, wisdom, and courage to do Your will in all things.

My Lord and my God, draw me close to You, nearer than ever before.

Amen.

WEEK FOUR

The Eucharist *and* History

A DIFFICULT TEACHING
DAY 22

"Live justly, love tenderly, and walk humbly with your God."
Micah 6:8

A few years ago, I wrote a book titled *Difficult Teachings*. The subtitle is *The 40 Most Challenging Teachings of Jesus*. Jesus didn't promise an easy life, but for 2,000 years people have been trying to combine Christianity with an easy life. They are incompatible. Not only did Jesus not promise an easy life, He promised us the opposite. When I reflect on these forty teachings now, I realize they are the teachings Christians have been avoiding since the beginning.

When Jesus was walking the dusty roads along the northwestern shore of the Sea of Galilee, His listeners struggled to understand and embrace some of His teachings more than others. But none more than the difficult teaching we are about to explore. More than any other teaching it was the one that His followers and critics alike struggled to get their hearts and minds around. Nothing has changed since then in this regard. It has been a source of controversy and division ever since.

"Jesus said to them, 'Truly, truly, I say to you, unless you eat the flesh of the Son of Man and drink his blood, you have no life in you; he who eats my flesh and drinks my blood has eternal life, and I will raise him up at the last day.'" (John 6:53–54)

This is a central moment in Jesus' public life. There are two moments when the people really struggled to understand what Jesus was saying. When Jesus explained that if they tore down the temple, He would rebuild it in three days, and what He is saying here about being the Bread of Life.

There are three other verses in this discourse that I would like to explore briefly with you, but it's worth reflecting on this whole section of John's Gospel. (John 6:22–71) It is rich with meaning and foreshadows not only the rest of Jesus' life, but also the life of the Catholic Church ever since.

How did the people respond? They had three reactions. Here is the first.

"The people then disputed among themselves, saying, 'How can this man give us His flesh to eat?'" (John 6:52)

We make so many assumptions and we believe our assumptions. But in truth, in most situations, we should question, challenge, and test our assumptions. Because the wrong assumptions make it impossible to reach valid conclusions. It's subtle, but do you see the assumption in the verse I just read? I'll share it again.

"The people then disputed among themselves, saying, 'How can this man give us His flesh to eat?'"

Did you catch it? "How can this man give us His flesh to eat?" They are operating under the assumption that Jesus is just a man, and that assumption makes it impossible for them to understand what Jesus is saying, never mind believe it.

If a homeless person tells you he is going to give you a letter of recommendation and a full scholarship to Harvard, you would naturally be skeptical and dismissive. That's the kind of situation that is playing out in this part of the Gospel. The people won't accept who Jesus really is, and so they are incapable of comprehending all He can do for them.

Then we move on to their second reaction. And this reaction is especially relevant today given all that is transpiring in our culture.

"Many of his disciples, when they heard it, said, "This is a hard saying; who can listen to it?" (John 6:60) Notice, they didn't say, "We don't understand" or even, "We don't want to live this teaching," or "Can you explain this a little more?" They didn't even want to listen to it.

They didn't even want to hear it.

This is the attitude of today's culture—and not only in relation to matters of faith. The poverty of mind and spirit has descended so low that this is now the attitude of the culture toward objective truths and scientific and biological realities.

For thousands of years a person who refused to acknowledge reality was considered a denialist and mentally ill. Today you can deny reality and be celebrated as enlightened. Is that not a sign that the culture itself is very sick indeed?

I was reading about mental illness recently for a project I am working on and came upon this description of schizophrenia, which is a tragic and desperately sad mental illness: "Schizophrenia is a serious mental health condition that causes disordered ideas, beliefs, and experiences. In a sense, people with schizophrenia lose touch with reality and do not know which thoughts and experiences are real and which are not."

It was the last line that got me thinking about today's culture. "People with schizophrenia lose touch with reality and do not know which thoughts and experiences are real and which are not." When we are not willing to even listen to the other side of an argument, we dangerously open ourselves to deception and tyranny of the worst kind. When a culture begins to deny objective reality, it is teetering on the edge of destruction.

To understand how far our culture has wandered from the Gospel, you only need to consider that objective truth cannot even be uttered in many situations today.

But we digress. The people's third reaction to Jesus' Bread of Life discourse was to abandon Jesus.

"After this many of His disciples drew back and no longer went about with Him." (John 6:66)

From the very beginning, the Eucharist has been a lightning rod, a point of contention and division. Regardless of what we have thought before or believe now, let us ask the Lord to open our hearts, minds, and souls to a deeper understanding of the Eucharist today, and with each passing day for the rest of our lives.

We are all hungry for something. Figuring out what we are really hungry for is one of the great spiritual quests of life.

There are so many different types of hunger. There is, of course, the natural hunger for food. Some people are hungry for comfort; others are hungry to belong; still others for success, safety, adventure, security, travel. To be human is to be hungry. Do you know what you are hungry for?

It takes an incredible spiritual awareness to work out over time what we are really hungry for. We may think that our hunger is for one thing, but once we have had our fill of that thing, we discover that the hunger is still there and deeper than ever.

What is the purpose of hunger? Every yearning we experience as human beings is a yearning for something more complete. The ultimate spiritual awareness leads us to understand that every yearning is in some mysterious way a yearning for God.

God speaks to us in our hunger. He uses our hunger to teach us and guide us. While we are searching far and wide in this world for something to satisfy our hunger, God is waiting to feed us the one thing that truly satisfies: Himself.

None of this is to say that physical hunger is unimportant. We have a legitimate need for nourishment. Many people in the world are desperately hungry for food and dismissing that need would be cruel and inhumane. God desires a world where everyone is physically well-fed, and we have a moral obligation to feed the hungry. But it is also true that our physical hunger is endless. You cannot eat enough hamburgers or rice or vegetables to never be hungry again. In just a few short hours, your body will begin to crave more nourishment.

Why does God make us this way? We cannot know the full reasons, but one explanation is that He knows we need constant reminders of our much deeper and more important spiritual hunger. Our constant physical hunger is meant to reveal our constant spiritual hunger for God. Each time our stomach growls, that is a reminder that our soul cries out for nourishment too. Our soul doesn't literally growl, but it does send us messages like: I want greater meaning. You have so much more to offer. There must be more to life. And the sad truth is that, for as many people who are physically hungry in the world, there are far more who are starving their souls.

But, unlike our physical hunger, this spiritual hunger does have a way to be perfectly and completely fulfilled. In John 6:35, Jesus speaks these words, "I am the bread of life; he who comes to me shall not hunger, and he who believes in me shall never thirst."

In the 2,000 years since Jesus spoke these words, they have not lost an ounce of relevance or power. Read them again. Do you feel your soul stirring? That's because they reveal a life-changing truth: God wants to feed your soul. He wants to feed you perfectly with Himself.

That is the beauty and power of the Eucharist.

So, let me ask you a question: What are you hungry for right now? What is God saying to you through your hunger? How is He using that hunger to lead you to Him?

Whether you are hungry for greater purpose in your life, a more fulfilling relationship, more meaningful work, rest, clarity, inspiration, joy, hope, peace—you won't be satisfied by the shallow things of the world. Jesus is waiting in the Eucharist to give you exactly what you need.

It's time to begin truly paying attention to the hunger in your soul. You can try to ignore it or deny it or pretend it isn't there, but it will never simply disappear. It is an invitation from God, and He will never cease trying to draw you to Himself.

The hunger in your soul is a good thing. Follow where it leads. Trust. Surrender. Believe. Receive.

LESSON

Only God can satisfy your endless longing. Allow Him to respond to your needs and feed you spiritually with the Eucharist.

VIRTUE OF THE DAY

Courage: The virtue of courage is moral strength in the face of danger or difficulty, especially in the face of anything that opposes our faith. Courage allows us to stand in our fears and do what is good, right, just, and noble. Everything significant in life requires courage.

SPIRITUAL COMMUNION

Jesus,
I believe that You are truly present
in the Most Holy Sacrament of the Eucharist.
Every day I long for more of You.
I love You above all things, and I desire to receive You into my soul.
Since I cannot receive You sacramentally at this moment,
I invite You to come and dwell in my heart.
May this spiritual communion increase my desire for the Eucharist.
You are the healer of my soul.
Take the blindness from my eyes,
the deafness from my ears,
the darkness from my mind,
and the hardness from my heart.
Fill me with the grace, wisdom, and courage to do Your will in all things.

My Lord and my God, draw me close to You, nearer than ever before. Amen.

THE LAST SUPPER
DAY 23

"Live justly, love tenderly, and walk humbly with your God."
Micah 6:8

Have you ever tried to get an obstinate child to take medication that you know will significantly help them? Did you know 42 percent of people who recover from a heart attack don't take their medication? More than 70 percent don't comply with doctor instructions generally after recovering from a life-threatening heart attack. Fallen human nature is real and everywhere. So, it's no wonder that we refuse to receive the spiritual medication God prescribes.

Our resistance to the Eucharist is staggering. The definition of obstinate is "stubbornly refusing" and sadly, tragically, this perfectly describes many people's relationships with the Eucharist.

If you ask people to name the most significant moments in history, most people won't even get close. The Last Supper is one that will be missing from most lists, and yet, if you remove it from human history everything changes.

The Institution of the Eucharist changed everything. And the Eucharist continues to change everything—if we will but cooperate and collaborate with God.

This was Saint John Vianney's observation, "There is nothing so great as the Eucharist. If God had something more precious, He would have given it to us."

If you knew you only had one night left to live, what would you do tonight?

You'd spend every moment possible with the people you love. You'd get your affairs in order spiritually. And you'd do whatever you could to ensure your nearest and dearest knew beyond a shadow of a doubt how much you love them.

The reality of death has that kind of effect. It clarifies. It makes our true priorities startlingly clear.

When it comes to Jesus, we have the unique case of the most significant person to ever live, the source of salvation for all the world, who knew exactly when and how He was going to die. We would be foolish not to look to the final days He spent on earth for clarity about what Jesus values above all else.

What did Jesus do on His final night on earth? The Gospels are aligned. Jesus gathered together His closest friends for the Last Supper and instituted the Sacrament of the Eucharist.

In the words of Saint Luke, "And when the hour came, he sat at table, and the apostles with him. And he said to them, 'I have earnestly desired to eat this Passover with you before I suffer.' And he took bread, and when he had given thanks he broke it and gave it to them, saying, 'This is my body which is given for you. Do this in remembrance of me.' And likewise the cup after supper, saying, 'This cup which is poured out for you is the new covenant in my blood.'" (Luke 22:14–16; 19-20)

Jesus knows He is going to die the very next day. In just a few short hours, Judas will betray Him. He knows that. His friends will scatter and abandon Him. He knows that. He will be brutally tortured and crucified. He knows that. He will die a gruesome death. He knows that.

When you know you are dying, it's not the moment to be cryptic, or mystical, or indirect. You wouldn't leave the doctor's office after a terminal diagnosis and draw up your Last Will and Testament with a bunch of metaphors and symbols and then say to your family, "I hope you figure out what I really mean!" No. You would be specific and clear.

Jesus was clear. "This is my Body. Eat it." And "This is my Blood. Drink it." "Do this in remembrance of me." It's not a symbol or a metaphor. It's a clear and direct command. Jesus impresses upon His disciples that this is a sacred meal of His Body and Blood and that they should continue this practice after He is gone.

The next time you are at Mass, simply allow yourself to be in the presence of God. Quiet your mind. Imagine yourself close to Jesus at the Last Supper. You are there during Jesus' final hours on earth. When the priest raises up the Host and says, "This is my Body, take and eat," let it sink in that Jesus is giving you the gift of His entire self. Will you give your entire self to Him?

Trust. Surrender. Believe. Receive.

LESSON

The Institution of the Eucharist changed everything. And the Eucharist continues to change everything—if we will but cooperate and collaborate with God. Resisting God is the antithesis of wisdom. In what ways are you resisting the good things God wants to share with you? Identify your spiritual needs and humbly ask God to satisfy them each time you receive the Eucharist.

VIRTUE OF THE DAY

Gratitude: The virtue of gratitude is simply about recognizing the good that is already yours. Practicing gratitude sensitizes us to all the blessings God has bestowed upon us. It is easy to overlook all the good in our lives and focus on what is frustrating or lacking. Thank every person who does even the slightest thing to assist you. And let your heart and mind be ever full of grateful prayers to God.

SPIRITUAL COMMUNION

Jesus,
I believe that You are truly present
in the Most Holy Sacrament of the Eucharist.

Every day I long for more of You.

I love You above all things, and I desire to receive You into my soul.

Since I cannot receive You sacramentally at this moment,

I invite You to come and dwell in my heart.

May this spiritual communion increase my desire for the Eucharist.

You are the healer of my soul.

Take the blindness from my eyes,

the deafness from my ears,

the darkness from my mind,

and the hardness from my heart.

Fill me with the grace, wisdom, and courage to do Your will in all things.

My Lord and my God, draw me close to You, nearer than ever before.

Amen.

THE EARLY CHRISTIANS
DAY 24

"Live justly, love tenderly, and walk humbly with your God."
Micah 6:8

For many years I have spent endless hours wondering what God's vision for the Church was in the beginning and what it is today. I have explored Catholic history and studied the roots of Christianity. I have also wondered what the essential differences are between Catholics today and the first Christians.

For the first Christians, Christianity was a lifestyle. They shared a common life. Living in community, they often worked together, prayed together, and studied the Scriptures together. Their faith was the center of their lives; it affected everything they did. They shared meals together, played together, and cared for each other in sickness. They allowed the principles of the Gospel to guide them in the activities of their daily lives. They comforted each other in their afflictions and challenged each other to live the Gospel more fully. There was unity and continuity between their professional lives and their family lives, between their social lives and their lives as members of the Church. They allowed the Holy Spirit to guide them in all they did. Then, at the pinnacle of their common life, they celebrated the Eucharist together.

This is what many writers would have you believe. But was it really like that? If you read Acts 2:43–47, and just these verses, you could be led to believe it. But the rest of Acts demonstrates that everything was not so idyllic among the first Christians.

The first deacons were chosen because the Gentile widows were not being cared for by the Jewish members of the Church. (Acts 6:1) There was conflict over how to treat the Gentiles. (Acts 15:1–21) Paul had to take Peter to task because he refused to eat with the Gentile converts. (Galatians 2:11–14) In his first letter to the Corinthians, Paul severely criticizes the community for selfishness, with the rich eating with their friends and the poor in their midst going hungry.

The first Christians were not perfect, but there was a real rigor among them for truth. It may not have been true of every member, but as a community they were rigorously seeking the best way to live the Christian life. Are you and I rigorously seeking the best way to live the Christian life?

Today, amid the busyness and complexities of modern life, the great majority of Catholics are challenged merely to make it to Mass each Sunday. In modern society, a great separation has taken place between the various aspects of our lives. Many people feel that they need to leave the values and principles of their faith outside certain activities in the same way you leave a coat in a waiting room. The modern world tries to separate faith from reason, the professional from the personal, the means from the ends. This separationist approach destroys unity of life and creates the modern madness of feeling torn in two, which we experience because our very nature tells us that we cannot divorce faith from reason, or the personal from the professional, or the means from the end. Living the Gospel is difficult; it always has been, and it always will be. This is what today's Catholics have in common with the first Christians, and with Christians of every place and time.

There has never been a time when the Church was the perfect society Jesus calls for us to be. There have been moments when certain individuals and communities have celebrated Christ's vision in awe-inspiring ways. But sustaining these moments is the real challenge. Think of how easy it is for you to turn your back on the-best-version-of-yourself. Consider how difficult it is for you to choose the-best-version-of-yourself in different situations each day. Now multiply that by 1.2 billion and you will have some sense of how difficult it is for the Church to be the-best-version-of-herself for even a single moment. Every time you engage in a self-destructive behavior, the Church becomes a-lesser-version-of-herself. And every time you bravely choose to become a-better-version-of-yourself, the Church becomes a-better-version-of-herself.

I don't know what the essential differences are between the first Christians and Catholics today. I do know that the ways of man will not get us from where we are today to where we are called to be. I also know that in every place and in every time since the Last Supper, Jesus has been present to guide you, me, and the whole Church through the Eucharist. I am certain that the Church needs less and less of your ideas and mine, and more and more guidance from Jesus Himself.

It is Jesus who will renew the world as we know it today. Will it happen with a blinding flash of light? I suspect not. The renewal that the Church and the world so desperately need at this moment in history will happen in this way: You and I will abandon the illusion of control and surrender our hearts to Jesus. We will allow Jesus to guide our words, thoughts, and actions one moment at a time. In this way, Jesus will slowly bring renewal to our lives, our marriages, our families, our businesses and schools, our parishes, our nations, our Church, and to all humanity.

Whatever the successes of the early Church, they were the fruit of their faithfulness to Jesus Christ under the inspiration of the Holy Spirit. Whatever the failures of the early Church, they were the result of rejecting Jesus. The same is true for you and me today.

Trust. Surrender. Believe. Receive.

LESSON

Humanity is in desperate need of God. The world is in desperate need of all the Church has to offer when it is thriving. The Catholic Church is in desperate need of renewal. Jesus wants to collaborate with you to bring that renewal about, so that together we can serve humanity in the powerful ways Jesus envisioned when He walked the earth 2000 years ago. But first, we need to abandon the illusion of control and surrender our hearts to Jesus.

VIRTUE OF THE DAY

Faithfulness: To be faithful means to be unfailingly loyal, reliable, and trustworthy. The virtue of faithfulness is an invitation to place Jesus at the center of our lives and protect His centrality against the constant temptation to place ourselves at the center of everything.

SPIRITUAL COMMUNION

Jesus,
I believe that You are truly present
in the Most Holy Sacrament of the Eucharist.
Every day I long for more of You.
I love You above all things, and I desire to receive You into my soul.
Since I cannot receive You sacramentally at this moment,
I invite You to come and dwell in my heart.
May this spiritual communion increase my desire for the Eucharist.
You are the healer of my soul.
Take the blindness from my eyes,
the deafness from my ears,
the darkness from my mind,
and the hardness from my heart.
Fill me with the grace, wisdom, and courage to do Your will in all things.
My Lord and my God, draw me close to You, nearer than ever before.
Amen.

EUCHARISTIC MIRACLES
DAY 25

"Live justly, love tenderly, and walk humbly with your God."
Micah 6:8

Once upon a time there was a priest who was plagued with doubts about whether Jesus was truly present in the Eucharist. . . until one day. After that day he never again doubted that Jesus was truly present in the Eucharist.

This opening may make this sound like a story, but it is a true story as we will soon discover, and there are more than a hundred like it that have been recognized by the Church.

Even though he was filled with doubts about the Real Presence of Jesus in the Eucharist, the priest faithfully celebrated Mass every day in fulfillment of his vocation.

On this particular day, around the year 700, in Lanciano, Italy, this priest was celebrating Mass in a small church and as he said the Words of Consecration ("Take this, all of you, and eat of it, for this is my Body which will be given up for you") the bread changed into living Flesh and the wine changed into Blood before his eyes.

Today, you can go to Lanciano and see the Flesh and Blood that has remained there for more than 1,300 years. The Flesh and Blood have been studied by scientists on a number of occasions, and the following conclusions have been drawn: The Flesh is real human flesh, and the Blood is real human blood. The Blood is type AB (the same in all approved Eucharistic miracles). The Flesh is muscular tissue from the heart. And there is no evidence of preservatives or any other chemical agents present.

Great faith and great doubt often go hand in hand, especially when it comes to accepting that Jesus is truly present in the Eucharist.

At times you may be fully convicted of this truth. As you approach the altar on Sunday, you feel fully aware and completely certain that it is really Jesus you are receiving. These are graced moments, and this kind of faith is a gift. At other times, you may think to yourself, "Is this really true? Is Jesus really there in that tiny white Host? Does this make any sense?" In these moments, you certainly aren't the first person to have doubts.

The Miracle of Lanciano is just one of more than a hundred Eucharistic miracles that have been documented throughout the life of the Church.

Many men and women have also been sustained by the Eucharist alone. Saint Catherine of Siena (1347–1380) lived the final seven years of her life consuming only the Eucharist and water. This had no effect on her energy, and in fact, many of her noteworthy accomplishments were achieved during this period.

On April 28, 2001, Eucharistic Adoration was being held at Saint Mary's parish in Chirattakonam, India. Suddenly, three red stains materialized on the Host. Amazed, the priest stored the Host carefully in the tabernacle. A few days later, he examined it to find the stains had arranged themselves to resemble the face of a man, which many have come to see as the face of Jesus. A photograph of the Host has inspired millions across the world.

On October 21, 2006, a parish in Tixtla, Mexico held a retreat. During Mass, two priests and a religious sister were handing out communion when the religious sister turned to the celebrant with tears in her eyes. The Host that she held was releasing a red substance. After medical testing, it was found to be human blood of AB type, just like at Lanciano.

It is easy to fall into the trap of placing these miracles in a far-off place with people you never knew. But it's important to remember what God is drawing our attention to through these miraculous stories. He performs miracles to show us the deeper spiritual reality at work in the circumstances of our lives.

Every Eucharistic miracle reveals the fact that just down the street at your local parish, each time the Mass is celebrated, the same miracle takes place. It happens in a way that isn't outwardly visible, but the bread and wine truly become the Body and Blood of Jesus.

These extraordinary reminders can assuage our doubts and open our hearts to the reality of Jesus' Real Presence in the Eucharist. But even more than that, if we open our hearts, these signs can deepen our awareness of the miracle of Jesus' presence all around us, not just at Mass, but in every moment of our lives.

Trust. Surrender. Believe. Receive.

LESSON

Great faith and great doubt often go hand in hand, especially when it comes to accepting that Jesus is truly present in the Eucharist. Ask Jesus to strengthen your faith in His True Presence in the Eucharist until it is unshakable.

VIRTUE OF THE DAY

Awe: The virtue of awe is a profound respect and reverence for the source of all life. Contemplation of life, truth, beauty, goodness and the sheer power of God all nurture the virtue of awe.

SPIRITUAL COMMUNION

Jesus,
I believe that You are truly present
in the Most Holy Sacrament of the Eucharist.
Every day I long for more of You.
I love You above all things, and I desire to receive You into my soul.
Since I cannot receive You sacramentally at this moment,

I invite You to come and dwell in my heart.

May this spiritual communion increase my desire for the Eucharist.

You are the healer of my soul.

Take the blindness from my eyes,

the deafness from my ears,

the darkness from my mind,

and the hardness from my heart.

Fill me with the grace, wisdom, and courage to do Your will in all things.

My Lord and my God, draw me close to You, nearer than ever before.

Amen.

YOUR FIRST COMMUNION
DAY 26

"Live justly, love tenderly, and walk humbly with your God."
Micah 6:8

Your First Communion was a historic event. As we explore the history of the Eucharist it is critically important to keep in mind that you have a place in that history, and it all began with your First Communion.

Some of us remember it, some of us don't. Some people have humorous stories to tell, and many people wish they had been better prepared. One of the best First Communion stories I have ever heard is by Sister Helena Burns in the book *Beautiful Eucharist*. The title of her story is "Why I Lied to My Pastor About First Communion." It is funny and profound, and a must read. But I digress.

The first time you received Jesus in the Eucharist was a historic moment. You stepped into a 2,000 year history of men and women participating in Eucharistic Glory. You became part of an eternal community that includes angels and saints who all come to the same table for this one meal. You received Jesus into your body and soul in the most intimate way possible for the first time.

Whether you receive the Eucharist for the first time at seven or seventy, that first time is just the beginning of the rest of your life. Every time you receive Jesus from that point forward, you have the chance to have a powerful encounter with the Alpha and the Omega.

Thérèse of Lisieux was intimately aware of this reality. She had been beautifully prepared for her First Communion by her parents who themselves became saints. She wrote a wonderful reflection on her own First Communion. It teaches us to make every encounter with Jesus count.

"At last the most wonderful day of my life arrived, and I can remember every tiny detail of those heavenly hours: my joyous waking up at dawn, the tender, reverent kisses of the other girls, the room where we dressed—filled with the white 'snowflakes' in which one after another we were clothed—and above all, our entry into chapel and the singing of the morning hymn: 'O Altar of God, Where the Angels are Hovering.'"

Nothing will transform your experience of the Eucharist like harnessing the power of anticipation. More than 50 percent of the joy in any great venture in life comes from anticipation. When you plan a great vacation, get ready for a first date, prepare for the birth of your child, so much of the joy comes before you ever even have the experience.

One of the greatest temptations around the Eucharist is to treat it like a regular part of our routine instead of the most significant moment of our week. And the way to move beyond that spiritual obstacle is to begin to build anticipation. Throughout the week, prepare for Mass by praying the Spiritual Communion each day, by reflecting on the Gospel for the coming Sunday's Mass, by fasting in order to intentionally become mindful of the hunger in your soul, and by arriving a few minutes early to quiet your heart, mind, body, and soul before Mass begins.

We prepare for everything we consider to be important in this life. Preparation builds anticipation. And anticipation fills our souls with joy. When we don't prepare for Mass, we reveal our misplaced priorities and rob ourselves of so much of the joy God wants to give us through the Eucharistic experience.

Trust. Surrender. Believe. Receive.

LESSON

You have a place in the history of the Eucharist. You have a place in the history of the Catholic Church. You have a place at

God's altar. Every invitation to receive Jesus is an immeasurable honor. Every encounter has the power to be life changing. Harness the power of anticipation by preparing for Mass.

VIRTUE OF THE DAY

Hope: The virtue of hope is a delicate combination of desiring eternal life and expecting it. It is one of the three theological virtues (of which God is the object): faith, hope, and love. Hope is a gift from God that leads us back to God. Repeat this simple prayer over and over throughout the day, "Lord, increase my hope."

SPIRITUAL COMMUNION

Jesus,

I believe that You are truly present
in the Most Holy Sacrament of the Eucharist.
Every day I long for more of You.
I love You above all things, and I desire to receive You into my soul.
Since I cannot receive You sacramentally at this moment,
I invite You to come and dwell in my heart.
May this spiritual communion increase my desire for the Eucharist.
You are the healer of my soul.
Take the blindness from my eyes,
the deafness from my ears,
the darkness from my mind,
and the hardness from my heart.
Fill me with the grace, wisdom, and courage to do Your will in all things.
My Lord and my God, draw me close to You, nearer than ever before.
Amen.

OUR LADY OF FATIMA
DAY 27

"Live justly, love tenderly, and walk humbly with your God."
Micah 6:8

The years was 1917. The world was at war. World War I was raging. Twenty million killed and twenty-one million wounded. And Mary came to warn people that even worse atrocities were coming if humanity didn't change course.

Three Portuguese children were the recipients of visions and messages from Mary. Lúcia; Francisco; and Jacinta, ages ten, nine, and seven. Fatima became the center of the world for many believers in 1917 and they flocked from far and wide hoping to experience one of the miracles or speak with the children.

Local authorities placed the children in three separate cells for three days, in an attempt to coerce them to recant their story. They told the children they would be fried in olive oil if they continued with their lies, and made all sorts of threats against their families and village. But the children held firm in their reports about what they had experienced.

What was the message? It was an urgent call to conversion and penance. This is the simplest way to state it. There were, of course, many aspects to the messages between May and October of 1917. Mary spoke about Heaven, Hell, Death and Judgment (the Four Last Things). The messages included insights about sin and sacrifice, and a call to pray the rosary for peace in our families and peace in the world. And of particular significance here on our journey toward Eucharistic Consecration, Mary spoke to the children and the world about respect for the Eucharist.

There have been many supernatural signs and apparitions throughout the course of Christian history, but none quite like

Fatima. It is without doubt the most prophetic of the modern apparitions. Mary gave the children a vision of Hell, foretold World War II (before the end of World War I) and predicted the immense damage Russia would do by abandoning the Christian faith and embracing Communism.

Mary presented two paths to the children: one of salvation and the other of destruction. The world didn't listen and everything Our Lady of Fatima predicted came to be, including the decimation of the Catholic Church from within. The world didn't listen. The world still isn't listening. Only 30 percent of Catholics in the United States believe Jesus is truly present in the Eucharist. The other 70 percent think it is just a symbol. Will you listen?

The first apparition took place on May 13, 1917. This was the feast of Our Lady of the Most Blessed Sacrament. Sixty-four years later on that day, Pope John Paul II was shot in Saint Peter's square. He prayed to Our Lady of Fatima the moment he was shot, and after recovering from his life-threatening injuries travelled to Fatima and placed the bullet the surgeon removed from his chest in the crown of the statue of Our Lady of Fatima.

The last apparition took place on October 13, 1917. Mary had told the children this would be the last apparition and promised a miracle that anyone in attendance would be able to witness. As many as 100,000 people were in the fields around Fatima that day and witnessed the Miracle of the Sun. It was reported on the front page of secular newspapers around the world the next day.

Witnesses tell the story of standing in the rain for hours, waiting for the final apparition and the promised miracle. The dark clouds that had filled the sky for most of the day parted and the sun appeared as an opaque spinning disc in the sky. Multicolored lights spread across the fields and the crowds. The sun, not as bright as usual, hurtled towards the earth before zig-zagging back to its normal position. Witnesses reported that they could stare at the sun on that day with no damage to their eyes. They also reported that the ground, which moments earlier had been wet and muddy, was now bone dry, as were their clothes, hair, and shoes.

Lúcia would later describe what happened on that October 13 in her memoirs. "Our Lady opened her hands and light streamed from them," she explained, "so intense that it penetrated their hearts and innermost souls. 'Who was that light?' we asked, falling to our knees, and repeating these words in our hearts: 'O most Holy Trinity, I adore you! My God, my God, I love you in the most Blessed Sacrament!'"

There are those who say we should not give too much attention to Mary as we should place our full attention on Jesus. Saint Maximilian Kolbe's insight was "Never be afraid of loving Mary too much. You can never love her more than Jesus did."

The one question I would like us to focus on in our reflection on the events and messages of Fatima is: How well do you receive the Eucharist? It can be done well, and it can be done poorly.

This question is "how well" not "how," but the two are related. How do you receive Communion? Some believe it doesn't matter what you wear, whether you kneel or stand, whether you receive on the tongue or in your hands, or if you whisper the 'Amen' or say it loudly. What matters is the disposition of your heart. If you have love and respect in your heart, then who cares what the mechanics of receiving are, they say. Others believe there is only one way to show proper respect for the Eucharist and to do anything else is irreverent.

The truth is, they're both right. How you receive outwardly matters. And how you receive outwardly should be an expression of your interior disposition. It's remarkable that the Maker of Heaven and Earth becomes present in the form of bread and wine and that you and I get to receive Him. It's the miracle of miracles. If we keep this in mind, "how" we receive Jesus will help us to receive the Eucharist "well"—internally and externally. The holiest external form loses significance if internally our hearts are turned away from God.

If you receive the Eucharist on the hands, you may have noticed that the Eucharistic Minister watches you until you consume the Host. Do you know why? Because Satanic cults and their worshippers understand who and what the Eucharist is. Their belief that Jesus is truly present in the Eucharist is unwavering. Satanists steal consecrated Hosts from Catholic churches and then mock Jesus and desecrate the Eucharist in a ceremony they refer to as a "Black Mass." This is why the Eucharistic Minister ensures you consume the Host.

Saint Paul taught that we should always receive Holy Communion in a worthy manner. He made it clear that if we receive the Eucharist in an unworthy way, then we eat and drink condemnation upon ourselves. (1 Corinthians 11:27–32)

One year before Mary appeared to the children of Fatima, God prepared the children with visits from the Angel of Peace. During one visit, he held a chalice with a Host suspended in the air over it. Leaving the chalice and Host suspended in the air, the angel knelt and had the children repeat three times:

"Most Holy Trinity, Father, Son and Holy Spirit, I adore you profoundly, and I offer you the most precious Body, Blood, Soul and Divinity of Jesus Christ, present in all the tabernacles of the world, in reparation for the outrages, sacrileges and indifferences by which he himself is offended. And, through the infinite merits of his Most Sacred Heart, and the Immaculate Heart of Mary, I beg of you the conversion of poor sinners."

Then the angel gave the Host to Lúcia and the Precious Blood to Jacinta and Francisco, and said: "Eat and drink the Body and Blood of Jesus Christ, terribly outraged by the ingratitude of men. Make reparation for their crimes and console your God."

I first visited Fatima in my early twenties. I felt a pull, a call to go there. Over the years since, I have visited many other sacred sites around the world, but I never felt that pull toward anywhere other than Fatima. In the ten years that followed my first pilgrimage to Fatima, I returned more than twenty-five times, bringing thousands of pilgrims to experience the mysteries of the place where Mary stood upon the earth to encourage and warn humanity.

Many years ago, I had the opportunity to attend Mass with Sister Lúcia. She was an old woman by then, living as a Carmelite in a cloistered community in Coimbra, just north of Fatima. I looked at her and wondered what she knew that the rest of us didn't. There was a peace and joy in her face, but also at moments, the anguish of someone who was carrying a heavy burden.

During my twenty-five visits to Fatima throughout my twenties, I spent countless hours in the Adoration Chapel asking for light and direction. Those were some of the best spent hours of my life.

Mary will always lead us to her Son. Pope Benedict XVI observed, "There is an indissoluble link between the Mother and the Son, generated in her womb by work of the Holy Spirit, and this link we perceive, in a mysterious way, in the sacrament of the Eucharist."

Mary will teach you to dedicate yourself to Jesus, she will lead you to consecrate your life to the Eucharist. There is nobody better to teach you how to dedicate yourself completely to Jesus in the Eucharist. She will lead you to Eucharistic Glory.

Let us strive to love Jesus in the Eucharist the way these simple children in Fatima did over one hundred years ago.

Trust. Surrender. Believe. Receive.

LESSON

We are all called to a continual conversion of the heart. Preparing to receive the Eucharist helps us to see ourselves as we really are. Receiving the Eucharist gives us the strength and courage needed to continually seek this conversion of the heart. Commit yourself not just to receiving Jesus in the Eucharist frequently but receiving Him well.

VIRTUE OF THE DAY

Fortitude: The virtue of fortitude is a moral virtue that ensures firmness in the face of difficulties and obstacles, and consistency in the pursuit of holiness. Deep, still waters in the soul are the gift of fortitude. This calmness of the soul is necessary to avoid getting carried away in the moment, and helps us to stay focused on our duties and commitments.

SPIRITUAL COMMUNION

Jesus,
I believe that You are truly present
in the Most Holy Sacrament of the Eucharist.
Every day I long for more of You.
I love You above all things, and I desire to receive You into my soul.
Since I cannot receive You sacramentally at this moment,
I invite You to come and dwell in my heart.
May this spiritual communion increase my desire for the Eucharist.
You are the healer of my soul.
Take the blindness from my eyes,
the deafness from my ears,
the darkness from my mind,
and the hardness from my heart.
Fill me with the grace, wisdom, and courage to do Your will in all things.

My Lord and my God, draw me close to You, nearer than ever before. Amen.

UNTIL THE END OF THE WORLD
DAY 28

"Live justly, love tenderly, and walk humbly with your God."
Micah 6:8

In 1163 a man was walking along the river Seine in Paris when he noticed a huge new building site. He approached the site and found men laying bricks. It was late in the afternoon, and the workers were tired and sweating.

He asked one worker, "What are you building here?" He replied, "I'm just laying bricks."

He asked another worker, "What are you building here?" The worker scoffed and said to the man, "Are you blind? I'm building a wall."

Frustrated, the man began to walk away, but as he turned, he bumped into one of the other workers, who was also laying bricks. "What are you building here?" he asked.

The builder stopped working. He stepped back and beckoned the man to do the same. Then, looking up toward the sky, he said, "We are building a cathedral."

"Cathedrals are beautiful," the man commented.

"You have never seen a cathedral this beautiful," the bricklayer replied. "This will be the finest cathedral the world has ever seen. It will tower above the city, men and women will marvel at it, and people will come from all over the world just to see it."

It took 182 years to finish that cathedral. Those who began building it never got to see it completed. It is 420 feet long, 157 feet wide, and 300 feet high, and with all of France's rich history, incredible sights, and phenomenal art, it is still the most visited attraction in France each year. With thirteen million annual visitors, that is almost twice as many as the Eiffel Tower and four million more than the Louvre.

It is the Notre-Dame Cathedral. Men and women of all faiths and no faith come to visit Notre-Dame de Paris and marvel at it.

I love Paris. I go there a couple of times a year for a week to get away from everything and everyone and focus on my writing. These trips usually correspond with starting and finishing a book. Each year my new book is released on August 15, the Marian Feast of the Assumption. But before the book is released to the public, I take the finished manuscript to Notre-Dame Cathedral and consecrate it to Mary's care.

On April 15, 2019, at about 6 P.M. I was sitting in my hotel room in Paris writing. I was finishing *Rediscover the Saints*. The city started going crazy. People were yelling and sirens started blaring, dozens of them. I looked out the window and saw smoke. Notre-Dame was on fire. I could see it from the window of my hotel room.

Notre-Dame Cathedral has long been considered one of the most beautiful places in the world. The world mourned as the iconic structure went up in flames. For hours, spectators kept watch in the streets, crying, praying, and singing hymns while one of the most beautiful churches in the world burned.

Before the fire, the Cathedral's breathtaking beauty had stood the test of time for over 800 years. The original construction began in 1163 and took nearly 200 years to complete. Thousands of workers contributed to erecting the massive structure, many of whom never saw it finished. It was a dangerous project, too. Estimates report somewhere between sixty to one hundred men died during construction. All the while, for generations, an unknown number of citizens gave money to sustain the project, often from their poverty. And after the fire, people from all over the world pledged nearly one billion dollars to rebuild it.

Because of the work, generosity, and sacrifices of so many,

millions of visitors and pilgrims have marveled at the Cathedral's Gothic beauty, and now, millions more will have the opportunity to do so for generations to come.

This all begs the question: Why? Why spend so much time, energy, and money to create one building? What motivated so many people to sustain such an effort over generations?

There are many possible motivations: aesthetics and architecture, legacy and vanity, ego and pride. Perhaps these all played some role. But each of these reasons pales in comparison to the deepest and most beautiful thing that motivated each block of limestone and each stroke of paint.

That reason? Faith. An unshakable belief that Jesus, truly present in the Eucharist, would come to dwell in the Cathedral for as long as it would stand.

Notre-Dame is just one example of literally thousands. Travel anywhere in the world and ask to be taken to the most beautiful building in the area. Most often, you will be taken to a Catholic church. Why have Catholics built so many beautiful churches in every century and all across the globe? I can tell you this: it's not about the art or the architecture. It's not about legacy or personal pride. It's because we believe that Jesus is truly present in the Eucharist.

Are there some ugly Catholic churches? Yes. Who built and designed them? It's only a guess, a speculation even, but I suspect they were built by people who didn't believe in the True Presence of Jesus in the Eucharist.

Stand in Saint Peter's Basilica in Rome, Saint Mary's Cathedral in Sydney, Duomo Cathedral in Milan, Las Lajas Sanctuary in Columbia, Saint Patrick's Cathedral in New York, the Basilica of the National Shrine of the Immaculate Conception in Washington DC, or any of a thousand other incredible Catholic churches around the world and you will experience a sense of the sacred and the awe it inspires.

What do these beautiful churches really say to us? They say that there is something greater here than art or architecture, something more than history—and not just something. . . but someone. That someone is Jesus Christ, truly present in the Eucharist, present in all these churches, and present in the tabernacle of your local church.

When Jesus was about to ascend into Heaven, He stood before His disciples and made an extraordinary promise: "I am with you always, to the end of the age." (Matthew 28:20) At the heart of the Catholic faith is an unwavering belief that Jesus fulfills this promise through the Eucharist. Not only does He remain with us in spirit, He stays with us physically by giving His Body and Blood in the Blessed Sacrament. The beauty of Catholic churches throughout the world is a testament to this faith. Right now, even as you read this, somewhere in the world, Mass is being celebrated and Jesus is once again making good on His promise.

What does this mean for you and me in our day to day lives? Well, if we accept this as true, then everything changes. When we have a question about our lives, we can no longer act as if we don't know where to find the answer. We can go to the One who has all the answers. When we are facing a dilemma we cannot solve, we can no longer say we have to solve it by ourselves. We can bring it to Jesus. When we are feeling lonely or distant from God, we can no longer say we don't know where to find Him. We can go to Mass or sit before the tabernacle.

Jesus chooses to be with us—body and spirit—in every tabernacle and on every altar in every Catholic church in the world. He promised to be with us until the end of the world—and He will never break that promise. The only question left is: Will we choose to be with Him?

Trust. Surrender. Believe. Receive.

LESSON

Jesus promised to be with us until the end of the world. He keeps that promise every day in the finest churches in the wealthiest cities and in the humblest churches in the poorest slums. Be mindful of His presence as you move about the world.

VIRTUE OF THE DAY

Sincerity: The virtue of sincerity involves being free from pretense, deceit, and hypocrisy. It is achieved by governing our words and actions with truth and justice. Keep your promises. If you say you will do something, do it.

SPIRITUAL COMMUNION

Jesus,
I believe that You are truly present
in the Most Holy Sacrament of the Eucharist.
Every day I long for more of You.
I love You above all things, and I desire to receive You into my soul.
Since I cannot receive You sacramentally at this moment,
I invite You to come and dwell in my heart.
May this spiritual communion increase my desire for the Eucharist.
You are the healer of my soul.
Take the blindness from my eyes,
the deafness from my ears,
the darkness from my mind,
and the hardness from my heart.
Fill me with the grace, wisdom, and courage to do Your will in all things.
My Lord and my God, draw me close to You, nearer than ever before.
Amen.

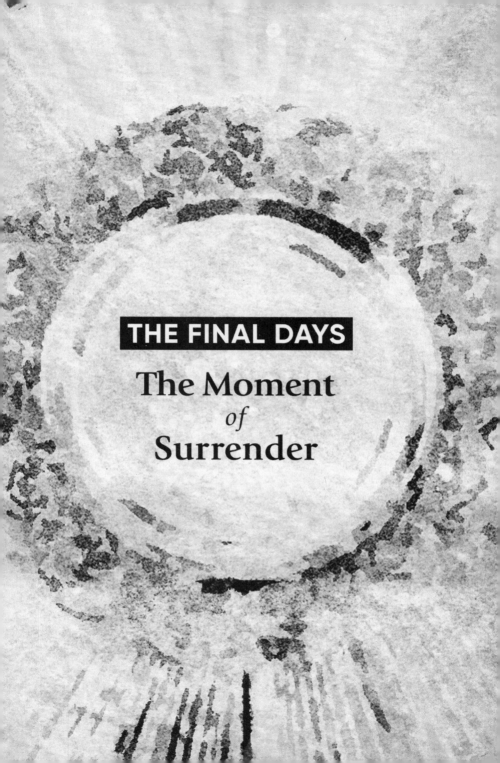

THE FINAL DAYS

The Moment *of* Surrender

CALLED TO HOLINESS
DAY 29

"This is the will of God, that you be holy."
1 Thessalonians 4:3

When you think about holiness, what comes to mind? Cabbage Patch Kids? Probably not.

An elderly priest named William Holt was walking across a busy street in the Upper East Side, when a photographer asked to take his photograph for his online blog, *Humans of New York*.

Fr. William agreed and the two men got talking. He had so many stories after decades of working with people.

"Do you have a favorite?" the photographer asked.

The old priest didn't have to think about it.

"Absolutely," he replied and launched straight into the story. "One Christmas there was a ten-year old girl from Ireland in my parish and she was dying of leukemia. All this girl wanted was a Cabbage Patch Doll. Ugliest doll you've ever seen in your life. On top of that they were seventy-five dollars. Seventy-five dollars! And to top it off, you couldn't get one, they were sold out everywhere.

"Her mother told me, 'I've looked in every store.'

"That same day a family from my parish asked what I wanted for Christmas. They had been very generous with me over the years, and I thought to myself, if anyone can get me one of these darn Cabbage Patch Kids it will be this couple.

"They could see me thinking and they added, 'We'd really like to do something special for you Father William.'

"I smiled. I knew they were going to think I was crazy. And then I replied, 'One Cabbage Patch Doll, and two walkie-talkies.'

"They looked at me baffled and said, 'Are you sure, Father?'

"'Yes, I'm sure. I was a kid once too!' I explained to them.

"A few days later a courier arrived at the door with exactly what I had asked for, one Cabbage Patch Doll and two walkie-talkies.

"The Cabbage Patch Doll went to the little girl. Then I gave one walkie-talkie to her and the other one to her twin brother, so they could speak while she was in isolation. She was dying, and it wasn't far off, and yet she was filled with a joy that I have rarely seen matched by anyone in this world.

"After she passed away, that little girl's mother wrote me a letter. It said: 'Thank you for your goodness, your thoughtfulness, your practical expression of God's love. Those walkie-talkies were the best medicine she ever had.'"

There are so many creative ways to walk the path of holiness. When Fr. William Holt's Holy Moment story was posted online the public's response was nothing short of incredible. The original post had thousands of comments, including the following:

"Where is your parish, Father? Your presence, your outlook, your optimism and kindness . . . that's the type of religion that I want to be part of."

"If this man had been my experience with religion, I might have stayed with it."

"Even someone like me who's not religious can see someone doing God's work and a kind heart."

"You are the epitome of what you stand for. You live it, not just preach it. Thank you. You've restored my faith."

"If all Christians were like him, I wouldn't be so resentful of Christianity."

"I love this so much. He really is bringing the love of God into the real-life struggles people have. He doesn't minimize their pain; he walks alongside them."

"I'm not religious, but this is the kind of Christianity I could actually embrace."

Each person who commented is essentially saying the same thing: If the religious people they knew, who claimed to love Jesus, had created more Holy Moments, these people would still be going to church.

As we begin these last few days of our journey toward consecration, I want to ensure that you are very clear about one thing: holiness is possible.

You are called to holiness and holiness is possible. God would not call you to something that you were incapable of living out. That would be reckless and cruel, and our God is not a reckless and cruel God. He is a God of mercy and compassion, a God who is careful and full of care.

Tomorrow we will learn how to collaborate with God to create Holy Moments like Father Holt did. Today, let's just cherish the thought that God wants us to live calm and holy lives in the midst of this chaotic world.

Think you can't? Those kinds of thoughts are only possible when you take the Eucharist out of the equation. Never take the Eucharist out of your equation.

"I can do all things through Christ who strengthens me." (Philippians 4:13) "For it is in Him that we live and move and have our being." (Acts 17:28)

Trust. Surrender. Believe. Receive.

LESSON
Love is creative. Holiness is creative. There are an infinite number of ways to share the love of God with the people who enter our lives.

VIRTUE OF THE DAY
Enthusiasm: The virtue of enthusiasm leads us not just to love God and neighbor, but to vigorously seek out opportunities to

do so. It reflects the state of a person's heart. Spiritual laziness leads to all manner of problems in this life and the next. Each day, choose a task that you have been avoiding or neglecting and attack it with new energy.

SPIRITUAL COMMUNION

Jesus,

I believe that You are truly present
in the Most Holy Sacrament of the Eucharist.
Every day I long for more of You.
I love You above all things, and I desire to receive You into my soul.
Since I cannot receive You sacramentally at this moment,
I invite You to come and dwell in my heart.
May this spiritual communion increase my desire for the Eucharist.
You are the healer of my soul.
Take the blindness from my eyes,
the deafness from my ears,
the darkness from my mind,
and the hardness from my heart.
Fill me with the grace, wisdom, and courage to do Your will in all things.
My Lord and my God, draw me close to You, nearer than ever before.
Amen.

HOLY MOMENTS
DAY 30

"This is the will of God, that you be holy."
1 Thessalonians 4:3

When I was fifteen years old, I had a great spiritual mentor. I don't know how my life would have unfolded if I hadn't met him. But it's difficult to imagine that life would have been anywhere near as fruitful or rewarding as it has been. He encouraged me to read the Gospels. He taught me how to pray. He showed me how to care for the poor and visit the lonely. He encouraged me to read great spiritual books. He watched without judgment as I foolishly wrestled with God. He listened patiently to my questions, doubts, excuses, and resistance. And perhaps most of all, he encouraged me to honor those sacred truths that were emerging in my soul: Something is missing, there is more to life, and you do have more to offer.

One of the fruits of this friendship was a moment of clarity so piercing that it has defined my life. I was walking home from meeting with him one day, when everything we had been discussing for months came together in a single clarifying thought: *Some moments are holy, some moments are unholy, and our choices can guide a moment in either direction.*

It was a rare moment of clarity in a chaotic and confusing world. It was also a moment of intense joy. Everything good in my life has been connected to that moment. And all the pain and disappointment I have caused myself and others has been the result of abandoning the wisdom that was revealed in that moment.

In that moment I realized what was possible. In that moment I learned to collaborate with God and create Holy Moments. It was a moment of grace like none other. And I have spent my life trying to help others discover that same clarity and joy. It is the only way I know to express my gratitude for the infinite blessings that moment brought to my life.

Now it's your turn. This is your moment. The moment when you realize that despite what your life has been up until now, and regardless of anything you have done in the past, what matters most is what you do next.

It's time for your life to make sense. Once we discover that some moments are holy, some moments are unholy, and our choices can guide a moment in either direction, life finally begins to make sense.

This is no small thing. Most people in the modern secular world cannot make sense of life. The culture has exiled them from God, religion, and spirituality. So, each day is a frustrated attempt to put together the jigsaw puzzle of life without crucial pieces. And the more disconnected from God our lives become, the more meaningless life becomes.

Holy Moments inject divine meaning and purpose into every moment of our lives. Meaning is crucial to our health and happiness. We cannot thrive as human beings without it. And we cannot live a meaningful life by filling our life with trivial things and meaningless activities. Holy Moments solve the meaninglessness of our lives.

Now, let us explore exactly how "our choices can guide a moment," for this is the essence of collaborating with God to create Holy Moments.

The crucial question is: What is a Holy Moment?

A Holy Moment is a single moment in which you open yourself to God. You make yourself available to Him. You set aside personal preference and self-interest, and for one moment you do what you prayerfully believe God is calling you to do.

These Holy Moments, these tiny collaborations with God,

unleash the pure unmitigated joy that I first experienced walking home that afternoon when I was fifteen. The same pure unmitigated joy that is about to flood every corner of your being.

So, begin today. One of the beautiful things about this idea is that you can implement it immediately. You do not need to study it for years. No special qualifications are necessary. You are equipped right now to collaborate with God and create Holy Moments. You know everything you need to know right now to begin activating Holy Moments in your life.

And here's the beautiful thing. If you can collaborate with God today to create one Holy Moment, you can create two tomorrow, and four the next day, and eight the day after that. There is no limit to the number of Holy Moments you can participate in. Holiness is possible.

Life all comes down to the moment of decision. Learn to master the moment of decision. We all make choices. That's the easy part. The hard thing about choices is living with them. We all have regrets. We have all said and done things that we would do differently if we could go back in time. We know we can't. We may have made peace with those choices to some extent, but still, in the quiet hours they haunt us.

If I could give only one piece of advice, it would be this: Make choices that are easy to live with. Make choices you can look back on longingly, like you do upon the best of times with the best of friends.

Life is choices. We are constantly making them. But are we choosing wisely? We are not born great decision makers. It is something that must be learned. The wisdom of Holy Moments will teach you how to become a great decision maker.

When you have a decision to make, consult your future self. Imagine yourself twenty years from now, looking back on this moment, and honor what your future self advises you to do.

Choices have consequences. It is one of life's fundamental truths. When we teach children that choices have consequences, the emphasis is usually placed on the consequences of poor choices, while the powerful and positive consequences of wise choices are often overlooked. Holy Moments are choices with powerful and positive consequences. Holy Moments are choices that are easy to live with.

It's time to start filling your life with Holy Moments. If you glance back at your life, the choices you find hardest to live with were unholy moments. And the choices you find easiest to live with, those you cherish, the ones you are rightly proud of, they each held the seed of goodness. They were Holy Moments.

Decision making is a powerful force in our lives. Our decisions quite literally shape our lives. We make the future with our choices. The beautiful thing about choices is you have more to make. Choices got you here, but if you don't like "here" all you need to do is start making different choices.

Your choices have power. If someone had an incredible power and used it for evil that would be a horrible thing. But what about if someone had an incredible power and didn't use it for good? There's something tragic and wrong about that too, isn't there?

That someone is you. You possess an incredible power. You can choose what is good and holy or you can choose what is unholy and destructive. Your choices have power.

So, let me ask you: What are you going to do with the rest of your life? More of the same? Continue to distract yourself with meaningless nonsense? Focus on what you can get? Keep dreaming about a change you know you will never make? Or are you finally, once and for all, ready to do something about the nagging dissatisfaction in your soul?

If you are ready for a change, it only takes a handful of Holy Moments to flood your soul with joy and show you a new and exciting vision of the rest of your life.

So, don't let your past rob you of your future. You are more than the worst thing that has ever happened to you. You are more than the worst thing you have ever done. God is never more than one choice away. It only takes one Holy Moment to shift the momentum of your life in the right direction.

Have you been wondering how you will live out this consecration for the rest of your life? One Holy Moment at a time.

Trust. Surrender. Believe. Receive.

LESSON

Some moments are holy, some moments are unholy, and you get to decide. Fill your life with Holy Moments, one at a time.

VIRTUE OF THE DAY

Simplicity: The virtue of simplicity fosters a spirit of contentment. Never confuse needs with wants. Concern yourself with the essential few rather than the trivial many. Liberate yourself from the things of this world so that your heart is free to rejoice in the pursuit of holiness.

SPIRITUAL COMMUNION

Jesus,
I believe that You are truly present
in the Most Holy Sacrament of the Eucharist.
Every day I long for more of You.
I love You above all things, and I desire to receive You into my soul.
Since I cannot receive You sacramentally at this moment,
I invite You to come and dwell in my heart.
May this spiritual communion increase my desire for the Eucharist.
You are the healer of my soul.
Take the blindness from my eyes,

the deafness from my ears,
the darkness from my mind,
and the hardness from my heart.
Fill me with the grace, wisdom, and courage to do Your will in all things.
My Lord and my God, draw me close to You, nearer than ever before. Amen.

THE WAY OF VIRTUE
DAY 31

"This is the will of God, that you be holy."
1 Thessalonians 4:3

Eight hundred years ago, a young Italian man searching for meaning in his life went into a dilapidated old church and heard the voice of God speak to him: "Rebuild my Church. As you can see, it is in ruins." If you and I listen carefully, I believe we will hear the same voice saying the same thing today.

The young man was Francis of Assisi. His first reaction was to repair and rebuild a number of churches in and around Assisi, but the voice kept calling to him: "Francis, rebuild my Church. As you can see, it is in ruins."

Over the past fifty years, we have spent a lot of time, energy, and money building and restoring the physical facilities of our churches. But the voice of God continues to call to us. Once again, God is saying, "Rebuild my Church," and the rebuilding that needs to be done now is of a spiritual nature.

The only way for our lives to genuinely improve is by acquiring virtue. Similarly, it is impossible for a society to genuinely improve unless its members grow in virtue. The renewal that the Church and society so desperately needs is a renewal of virtue. And it is our relationship with Jesus that gives us the strength, the grace, and the wisdom to grow in virtue.

What is virtue? It is "a habitual and firm disposition to do good." (CCC 1833)

The great fallacy of the lukewarm moral life is to believe that our sole responsibility is to eliminate vice from our lives. In the absence of a sincere and focused effort to grow in virtue and an openness to God's will for our lives, vice will creep into our lives in the form of a hundred different self-centered and self-destructive habits.

No man or woman is born virtuous. Good habits are not infused. Virtue must be sought out and can be acquired only by continual practice. You learn to ride a bicycle by riding a bicycle. You learn to play baseball by playing baseball. You learn to be patient by practicing patience.

You become virtuous by practicing virtue.

For thousands of years, politicians, philosophers, and priests have all argued about the best way to organize society. Many organizing concepts, including duty, obligation, law, force, obedience, tyranny, and greed have been employed throughout history by various societies and organizations. But what is the ultimate organizing principle? It is virtue. Two virtuous people will always have a better relationship than two people without virtue. Two patient people will always have a better relationship than two impatient people. Two kind and generous people will always have a better relationship than two selfish people. Two humble people will always have a better relationship than two proud people. Not sometimes, but every single time. And the world is just an extension of your relationship with me and my relationship with you. If we are both striving to live virtuous lives, our relationship will prosper. But when we give up our striving for virtue, our relationship will disintegrate.

Virtue leads to better people, better living, better relationships, and a better world. If humanity is to flourish in the twenty-first century it will be because we realize once and for all that the key organizing concept of a truly great civilization is virtue.

The connection between virtue and the flourishing of an individual is unquestionable. To live a life of virtue is to move beyond the restlessness and chaos that agonize the human heart and embrace a life of order and coherence.

The Church has always proclaimed that the seven foundational virtues are the cornerstone of the moral life. This foundation is made up of the supernatural virtues (Faith, Hope, and Love) and the four cardinal virtues (Prudence, Justice, Temperance, and Fortitude). The supernatural virtues free us from self-centeredness, protect us from the ultimate vice—pride—and dispose us to live in relationship with God. The cardinal virtues, which are sometimes referred to as "the human virtues," allow us to acquire the self-mastery necessary to make us free and capable of love. They do this by ordering our passions and guiding our conduct in accordance with faith and reason. (CCC 1834)

The only way for our lives to genuinely improve is by acquiring virtue. To grow in virtue is to improve as a human being. To become a better person today than I was yesterday, this is accomplishment. Ernest Hemingway observed, "There is nothing noble in being superior to your fellow man; true nobility is being superior to your former self."

Virtue is central to the growth of a Christian. Earlier in our journey together (Day 8) we discussed how people tend to emulate the five people they spend most time with. Are your five people virtuous people? If not, you need to make a change. And you may be thinking, "I can't make a change. My five people are set, and they are not virtuous."

But let's think back to something else we have learned on this pilgrimage together. Don't let what you can't do interfere with what you can do (Day 21). The devil wants you to focus on what's not possible. Jesus helps us to focus on what is possible and find new possibilities.

Maybe the people around you have no interest in virtue. But I look across my bookshelf and I see plenty of virtuous people you can spend time with: Mother Teresa, Fulton Sheen, C.S. Lewis, Teresa of Ávila, Thérèse of Lisieux, Augustine, Aquinas, Chesterton, Tolkien, Kreeft, Dorothy Day. The list is endless. Virtues are the habits of the saints. And then, of course, there is Jesus in the Eucharist.

Jesus is virtue personified. He is honest, patient, kind, humble, courageous, compassionate, hopeful, wise, generous, gentle, resilient, loving. And whenever we act virtuously, we, in some mysterious and amazing way, usher God's grace and goodness into the world. Virtue became man so that man could become virtue.

The Eucharist is, as Saint Peter Eymard observed, "a divine storehouse filled with every virtue; God has placed it in the world so that everyone may draw from it." So, draw from it. Spend time with Jesus in the Eucharist and draw from that storehouse abundantly and often.

Trust. Surrender. Believe. Receive.

LESSON

To live a life of virtue is to move beyond the restlessness and chaos that agonize the human heart and embrace a life of order and coherence. There is a clear connection between a life of virtue and human flourishing. Virtue leads to better people, better living, better relationships, and a better world. The Eucharist is a divine storehouse filled with every virtue. The more time we spend with Jesus in the Eucharist, the more abundantly we can draw virtue from that storehouse.

VIRTUE OF THE DAY

Generosity: The virtue of generosity mirrors the abundance of God's generosity. Give something away every day. It need not be a material possession or money. Give a compliment, a smile, advice, encouragement. Express your appreciation. Catch someone doing something right. Give everywhere you go to everyone you meet. Live a life of staggering generosity.

SPIRITUAL COMMUNION

Jesus,

I believe that You are truly present

in the Most Holy Sacrament of the Eucharist.

Every day I long for more of You.

I love You above all things, and I desire to receive You into my soul.

Since I cannot receive You sacramentally at this moment,

I invite You to come and dwell in my heart.

May this spiritual communion increase my desire for the Eucharist.

You are the healer of my soul.

Take the blindness from my eyes,

the deafness from my ears,

the darkness from my mind,

and the hardness from my heart.

Fill me with the grace, wisdom, and courage to do Your will in all things.

My Lord and my God, draw me close to You, nearer than ever before.

Amen.

THE PRESENTATION OF JESUS
DAY 32

"This is the will of God, that you be holy."
1 Thessalonians 4:3

"When the time came for their purification according to the law of Moses, they brought him up to Jerusalem to present him to the Lord (as it is written in the law of the Lord, 'Every first-born male shall be designated as holy to the Lord'), and they offered a sacrifice according to what is stated in the law of the Lord, 'a pair of turtledoves or two young pigeons.'

"Now there was a man in Jerusalem whose name was Simeon; this man was righteous and devout, looking forward to the consolation of Israel, and the Holy Spirit rested on him. It had been revealed to him by the Holy Spirit that he would not see death before he had seen the Lord's Messiah. Guided by the Spirit, Simeon came into the temple; and when the parents brought in the child Jesus, to do for him what was customary under the law, Simeon took him in his arms and praised God, saying, 'Master, now you are dismissing your servant in peace, according to your word; for my eyes have seen your salvation, which you have prepared in the presence of all peoples, a light for revelation to the Gentiles and for glory to your people Israel.'

"And the child's father and mother were amazed at what was being said about him. Then Simeon blessed them and said to his mother Mary, 'This child is destined for the falling and the rising of many in Israel, and to be a sign that will be opposed so that the inner thoughts of many will be revealed—and a sword will pierce your own soul too.'

"When they had finished everything required by the law of the Lord, they returned to Galilee, to their own town of Nazareth.

The child grew and became strong, filled with wisdom; and the favor of God was upon Him." (Luke 2:22–35, 39–40)

Have you ever waited for something with great anticipation? Did you wait patiently? What are you waiting for in your life right now?

Simeon had waited. This was his moment. He had waited patiently, and he had prayed patiently. Now he took baby Jesus in his arms. Imagine the emotion as he pulled the child to his chest, his long gray beard caressing the child's head. His face filled with a strange combination of joy and anguish—joy for the present, anguish for the future he knew or sensed the child would face. The tears streaming down his face.

Put yourself there in the temple that day. Mary and Joseph have brought Jesus to present Him to the Lord in obedience to the Jewish law. Mary, the Mother of God, submits her child to the Law of Moses. Think about it: They are presenting God to God, and yet they are obedient to the law. If anyone was ever exempt from a law, it was Jesus, Mary, and Joseph in this moment. But they chose obedience. This is a momentous act of humility.

How often do we decide that a particular rule or law doesn't apply to us? When we drive faster than the speed limit, neglect to declare some taxable income, or leave our phones on when they should be turned off, we are really saying, "That law doesn't apply to me. That's for everyone else. I am above that law." This is our arrogance.

"Poverty, chastity, and obedience. Obedience is by far the hardest to live," a wise old monk once told me. To whom are you willing to be obedient? We are allergic to the very word. It seems we are obedient only to our own desires. Addicted to comfort and convenience, we reject the very notion of obedience. No wonder we have such a hard time surrendering in obedience to the will of God.

The word obedience comes from the Latin word obedire, which means "to listen deeply." Mary listened deeply. Simeon listened deeply. By listening deeply, they saw the wisdom of God's way.

With these inspirations in our hearts and minds, we turn to Jesus and pray:

Lord, give us the patience of Simeon, knowing that our impatience gets in the way of obedience; give us the grace necessary to see obedience as something that is life-giving rather than something oppressive. Help us to become a little more patient each day and light a flame of desire for obedience in our hearts.

Inspire us to realize that Your guidance, rules, and laws are designed in part to protect us from the great misery people experience when they reject Your wisdom. And knowing that we cannot love you if we are not obedient to You, we present ourselves to You today just as Mary and Joseph presented Jesus.

Instruct us in all things; guide us in all things; command us in all things; we desire to be Your faithful servants.

Mary, pray for us and teach us to listen deeply to your Son.

Amen.

Are you ready? I think you are. Just as Joseph and Mary presented Jesus in the temple, tomorrow you will consecrate yourself and your life to Jesus in the Eucharist. This will be an epic moment in your life. Consecration to the Eucharist will change you in ways that you cannot even begin to understand. And so, my advice to you today is simple and practical: Tomorrow's going to be a momentous day, get to bed early and get a good night's rest.

Trust. Surrender. Believe. Receive.

LESSON

Learn to listen deeply to the voice of God in your life. Our desire to direct our own actions is born from ignorance and arrogance. Obedience to the will of God is the life-giving path to flourishing and become all God created you to be. Try it in some small moments and feel your soul begin to fill with joy. This will give you the courage to surrender to His will more with every passing day.

VIRTUE OF THE DAY

Obedience: The virtue of obedience is simply doing what God asks, even when you would prefer to do something else, or think there is a better way. Obedience to God and obedience to a virtue-seeking earthly authority are both profound blessings that liberate the soul and make the peaceful acceptance possible.

SPIRITUAL COMMUNION

Jesus,
I believe that You are truly present
in the Most Holy Sacrament of the Eucharist.
Every day I long for more of You.
I love You above all things, and I desire to receive You into my soul.
Since I cannot receive You sacramentally at this moment,
I invite You to come and dwell in my heart.
May this spiritual communion increase my desire for the Eucharist.
You are the healer of my soul.
Take the blindness from my eyes,
the deafness from my ears,
the darkness from my mind,
and the hardness from my heart.
Fill me with the grace, wisdom, and courage to do Your will in all things.
My Lord and my God, draw me close to You, nearer than ever before.

TOTALLY YOURS
DAY 33

"I will give thanks to you Lord with my whole heart."
Psalm 9:2

"This is the day the Lord has made, let us rejoice and be glad." This is my spontaneous prayer as I get out of bed each morning. I'm not sure how it started or when it began, but there is something about this verse that fills my soul with joy. Perhaps it is the hope of a new beginning, maybe it is anticipation of unexpected blessings. I'm not sure.

Today is the end of your journey. We have been on this path together for thirty-three days. Congratulations! You did it. I am sure there are many who didn't make it. We pray they will set back on the path and complete this Eucharistic Consecration soon. But today is your day. I hope you will find a way to celebrate it.

Totus Tuus. This is a Latin phrase which means "totally yours." It was the motto of Pope John Paul II and signifies a radical commitment to Jesus through Mary. Today you are saying to Jesus, "I am totally Yours and everything I have is Yours."

This total self-giving is something we have witnessed at every Mass we have ever attended. In the Eucharist, Jesus gives His whole self to us completely and absolutely. And now, in this Eucharistic Consecration, we respond with love and generosity by pledging our whole selves to Jesus in the Eucharist.

This consecration is a radical act of love. It is a radical act of generosity. Deep down we all desire to make the radical and complete gift of self that you are going to make to God today.

Saint Anthony of Padua advises you today, "By his whole self He redeemed your whole self, so that He alone might possess you wholly. Therefore, love the Lord your God with all your heart.

Do not withhold part of yourself... Love wholly, not in part."

Today you are offering your whole self to Jesus in the Eucharist. Don't hold anything back. Your consecration is a declaration before God.

You are joining your "yes" with Mary's "yes."

You are joining your "yes" with Joseph's "yes."

You are joining your "yes" with the "yes" of Peter and Paul.

You are joining your "yes" with the "yes" of Michael, Gabriel, and Raphael, John the Baptist, Andrew, James, John, Thomas, James, Phillip, Bartholomew, Matthew, Simon, Jude, Matthias, Barnabas, Luke, and Mark.

You are joining your "yes" with the "yes" of Francis, Augustine, and Aquinas.

You are joining your "yes" with the "yes" of Mother Teresa and John Paul II.

You are joining your "yes" with the "yes" of Teresa of Ávila and Thérèse of Lisieux.

You are joining your "yes" with the "yes" of all of God's holy angels and saints.

This is a historic moment. An epic moment in your spiritual journey.

You will receive many gifts from this Eucharistic Consecration. One of those gifts will be clarity. Commitment leads to clarity. And clarity allows us to focus our attention and energy on those things that are most important. The clarity of commitment is a thing of beauty, profound and at the same time intensely practical. You will see with new eyes what matters most and what is shallow, superficial, and insignificant. Cherish that clarity. It is a rare gift in a world drowning in chaos and confusion.

There is a phrase in Luke's Gospel that I want you to delve into over the next several days. It is one of my favorite lines in the Scriptures. It was on the night Jesus was born. The Shepherds and angels and Magi were saying all these amazing things about who Jesus was and what He was going to do for humanity. And the Scripture reads, "And Mary treasured all these words and pondered them in her heart." (Luke 2:19)

There are words from these thirty-three days for you to treasure. There are words you will receive from God today as part of your consecration that you will want to ponder in your heart for days and weeks, and months and years to come. I hope you will gift yourself the time needed to do that pondering. I pray you continue to unpack the ideas God has filled your heart, mind, and soul with during these thirty-three days.

The final piece of our journey together is the actual Prayer of Consecration. But to prepare our hearts and minds to conceive what is about to happen, I would like to share with you a poem and the story about how it came into my life. It describes what is about to happen to you better than I ever could.

My fourth-grade teacher, Mrs. Pauline Rutter, in her wisdom, introduced my classmates and me to the following poem. After reciting it one day, she announced that over the next week, we were all to learn the poem by heart. Then each morning, to begin our day, someone would recite the poem for the class. It was just one example of her many moments of genius. At the time, our understanding of it was shallow, perhaps because one needs to experience some of life's hard knocks to truly appreciate the full meaning.

'Twas battered and scarred and the auctioneer
Thought it scarcely worth his while
To waste much time on the old violin,
But held it up with a smile.
"What am I bidden, good folks" he cried,
"Who'll start the bidding for me?"

"A dollar, a dollar" Then two! Only two?
"Two dollars and who'll make it three?"

"Three dollars, once; three dollars twice;
Going for three . . ." But no,
From the room, far back, a grey-haired man
Came forward and picked up the bow;
Then wiping the dust from the old violin,
And tightening the loose strings
He played a melody pure and sweet
As a caroling angel sings.

The music ceased, and the auctioneer,
With a voice that was quiet and low,
Said: "What am I bid for the old violin?"
And held it up with the bow.
"A thousand dollars, and who'll make it two?
Two thousand! And who'll make it three?
Three thousand, once; three thousand twice,
And going and gone," said he.

The people cheered, but some of them cried,
"We do not quite understand.
What changed its worth?" Swift came the reply:
"The touch of a Master's hand."

And many a man with life out of tune,
And battered and scarred with sin,
Is auctioned cheap to the thoughtless crowd
Much like the old violin.

A "mess of pottage," a glass of wine,

A game—and he travels on.
He is "going" once, and "going" twice,
He's "going" and almost "gone."
But the Master comes, and the foolish crowd
Never can quite understand
The worth of a soul and the change that is wrought
By the touch of the Master's hand.

"The Touch of the Master's Hand" by Myra B. Welch.

Amazing things become possible when we place ourselves in the Master's hands, and that is exactly what you are going to do today by consecrating yourself to Jesus in the Eucharist.

You may feel battered and scarred. You may think your life is out of tune. You may have lost sight of your true worth. The thoughtless crowd may have given up on you. But when we allow the Master to direct our lives, everything changes.

Throughout this journey I have been speaking of Eucharistic Glory. So, you are no doubt wondering, what is Eucharistic Glory?

We pray in the Mass, "All glory and honor be yours forever and ever. Amen." It comes from the Book of Revelation. (5:13) But God wants us to share in His glory. *The Catechism of the Catholic Church* teaches us that the Eucharist is a pledge of our future glory with Him.

"Having passed from this world to the Father, Christ gives us in the Eucharist the pledge of glory with Him. Participation in the Holy Sacrifice identifies us with his Heart, sustains our strength along the pilgrimage of this life, makes us long for eternal life, and unites us even now to the Church in Heaven, the Blessed Virgin Mary, and all the saints." (CCC 1419)

"Unites us even now to the Church in Heaven." Every time we receive Jesus in the Eucharist, we touch Heaven, we are joined with all the angels and saints, and in that moment, we share in the glory of God—that is Eucharistic Glory.

Heaven and Earth meet in the Eucharist. It's time to discover all that you are, all that you can be, and all that you will be in Jesus Christ. It's time to embrace Eucharistic Glory.

And now, it is time to consecrate yourself to Jesus Christ in the Eucharist . . .

PRAYER OF EUCHARISTIC CONSECRATION

Lord Jesus Christ,
Bread of Life,
True God and True Man,
The Alpha and the Omega,
Truly present—Body, Blood, Soul, and Divinity—in the Blessed Sacrament,
I consecrate myself to You today without reservation.

Here I am, Lord.
I come to do Your will.
Come and dwell within me.
Heal my body,
focus my mind,
transform my heart,
and nourish my soul,
so that I may represent You faithfully in the many situations and circumstances of my daily life.

Lord Jesus Christ, truly present in the Eucharist,
I consecrate myself to You today without reservation.
I hold nothing back.
I surrender completely and absolutely to Your goodness.
I know the plans You have for me:
Plans for prosperity and well-being,
plans for good and not evil,
plans that give me hope and a future.

Lord Jesus Christ, truly present in the Eucharist,
I consecrate myself to You today without reservation.

I surrender my whole being to Your care.
I surrender my life, my plans, and my very self to You.
I place all that I am at Your feet.
I place all that I have at Your feet.
Take what You want to take and give what You want to give.

Lord Jesus Christ, truly present in the Eucharist,
I consecrate myself to You today without reservation.
Transform me.
Transform my life.
I trust in the eternal genius of Your ways.
I make myself 100 percent available to You.
Lead me, encourage me, challenge me.
Show me how I can collaborate with You,
and I will do what You ask with a joyful heart.

Lord Jesus Christ, truly present in the Eucharist,
I consecrate myself to You today without reservation.
Grant me the grace, wisdom, and courage,
to live justly,
love tenderly,
and walk humbly with You, my God,
all the days of my life.

Angels and Saints,
Lead me in the ways of the pilgrim,
so that one day I too may share in Heaven.
With His blessing and by His grace,
bestow upon me your humility, generosity, and devotion,
and I implore you to carry this prayer to our Eucharistic Lord.

Mary, Mother of Jesus,
Teach my soul how to receive your Son in the Eucharist,
and how to represent Him in this world.
Teach me the surrender and sacrifice that were necessary
to make the Eucharist possible in this broken world.
Intercede for me and obtain the grace necessary
to allow your Son's teachings to penetrate
the darkest, coldest, hardest parts of my heart,
so that by receiving Him in the Eucharist
my heart may become ever more like His Eucharistic Heart.

Amen.

APPENDIX

CONSECRATE AMERICA TO THE EUCHARIST

WE DREAM OF CONSECRATING THE WHOLE WORLD TO THE EUCHARIST.

One person at a time,
one marriage at a time,
one family at a time,
one neighborhood at a time,
one parish at a time,
one diocese at a time,
one country at a time.

IMAGINE THE WHOLE WORLD CONSECRATED TO JESUS IN THE EUCHARIST.

Join us in this dream and together we can do something bold for God. To learn more about how you can get involved, visit: Eucharist.us

Catholics have consecrated themselves to the Immaculate Heart of Mary, to the Sacred Heart of Jesus, to Saint Joseph, Saint Raphael, Saint Michael the Archangel, Saint Anne, the Holy Spirit, the Miraculous Medal, Our Lady of Guadalupe, the Mediatrix of All Grace, Our Lady of Fatima, Our Lady of Lourdes, Our Lady of Czestochowa, Our Lady of Mount Carmel, Our Lady of Sorrows, and to the Holy Trinity.

I believe it is time we consecrated ourselves to Jesus in the Eucharist—it is time for a Eucharistic Consecration.

To learn more about our hopes to have your parish and diocese consecrated to the Eucharist:

Eucharist.us

BECOME A EUCHARISTIC MISSIONARY

Would you like to help us coordinate our efforts in your community? Are you interested in leading small groups through *33 Days to Eucharistic Glory*? Would you like to learn more about our neighborhood evangelization? Would you like to help consecrate your parish and diocese to the Eucharist?

Consider joining one of the most passionate groups of Catholics in the world by becoming a Eucharistic Missionary. You don't need to travel to foreign lands to become a missionary, your missionary efforts are needed right here at home.

We would love to partner with you.

To learn more, visit:

Eucharist.us

FEAST DAY TABLES

2024

BEGIN PREPARATION	FEAST OF JESUS	CONSECRATION/ FEAST DAY
January 1	The Presentation of the Lord	February 2
February 21	Palm Sunday	March 24
February 26	Good Friday	March 29
February 28	Easter	March 31
March 6	Divine Mercy Sunday	April 7
April 10	The Ascension of the Lord	May 12
April 24	Trinity Sunday	May 26
May 1	Corpus Christi	June 2
May 6	Feast of the Sacred Heart of Jesus	June 7
July 5	The Transfiguration of the Lord	August 6
August 13	The Exaltation of the Holy Cross	September 14
October 23	Solemnity of Christ the King	November 24
November 23	Christmas	December 25
November 27	The Holy Family of Jesus, Mary, and Joseph	December 29
December 4, 2024	The Epiphany of the Lord	January 5, 2025
December 11, 2024	The Baptism of the Lord	January 12, 2025

FEAST DAY TABLES

2025

BEGIN PREPARATION	FEAST OF JESUS	CONSECRATION/ FEAST DAY
January 1	The Presentation of the Lord	February 2
March 12	Palm Sunday	April 13
March 17	Good Friday	April 18
March 19	Easter	April 20
March 26	Divine Mercy Sunday	April 27
April 30	The Ascension of the Lord	June 1
May 14	Trinity Sunday	June 15
May 21	Corpus Christi	June 22
May 26	Feast of the Sacred Heart of Jesus	June 27
July 5	The Transfiguration of the Lord	August 6
August 13	The Exaltation of the Holy Cross	September 14
October 22	Solemnity of Christ the King	November 23
November 23	Christmas	December 25
November 26	The Holy Family of Jesus, Mary, and Joseph	December 28